THOMAS MANTON

The Guided Tour Series

Anne Bradstreet: A Guided Tour of the Life and Thought of a Puritan Poet, by Heidi L. Nichols

J. Gresham Machen: A Guided Tour of His Life and Thought, by Stephen J. Nichols

Jonathan Edwards: A Guided Tour of His Life and Thought, by Stephen J. Nichols

Katherine Parr: A Guided Tour of the Life and Thought of a Reformation Queen, by Brandon G. Withrow

Martin Luther: A Guided Tour of His Life and Thought, by Stephen J. Nichols

Pages from Church History: A Guided Tour of Christian Classics, by Stephen J. Nichols

Thomas Manton: A Guided Tour of the Life and Thought of a Puritan Pastor, by Derek Cooper

Stephen J. Nichols, series editor

THOMAS MANTON

*A Guided Tour of the Life and
Thought of a Puritan Pastor*

DEREK COOPER

P U B L I S H I N G
P.O. BOX 817 • PHILLIPSBURG • NEW JERSEY 08865-0817

Page design by Lakeside Design Plus

Printed in the United States of America

Library of Congress Cataloging-in-Publication Data

Cooper, Derek, 1978-
  Thomas Manton : a guided tour of the life and thought of a Puritan pastor / Derek Cooper.
      p. cm. -- (The guided tour series)
  Includes bibliographical references (p.   ) and indexes.
  ISBN 978-1-59638-213-8 (pbk.)
  1. Manton, Thomas, 1620-1677. 2. Puritans--England--Clergy--Biography.
I. Title.
  BX9339.M36C66 2011
  285'.9092--dc23
  [B]
                                        2011031327

Dedicated to Steve Nichols

CONTENTS

List of Illustrations   9

Foreword by Carl Trueman   11

Acknowledgments   13

Part One: Manton in Context: A Seventeenth-Century English Preacher

1. The Servitor from Somerset, 1620–40   19

2. The London Presbyterian, 1640–56   39

3. The King of Preachers, 1656–77   59

Part Two: Manton as Biblical Interpreter: His Commentary on James

4. Manton and the Reformers on James 1:1: Jostling James into the Canon   83

5. Manton and the Puritans on James 2:14–26: Saving the Strawy Epistle   101

6. Manton and the Anglicans on James 5:14–16: Settling the Sacraments   121

**Part Three: Manton as Public Preacher:
Selected Sermons**

7. Manton as Minister: Learning How to
    Meditate   145

8. Manton as Public Figure: Living as a
    Christian Citizen   167

9. Manton as Preacher: Learning about Jesus and
    His Call to Denial   191

**Appendices: Continuing the Journey:
Manton's Legacy and Works**

Appendix A: Manton's Legacy: Puritan, Preacher,
    Public Theologian   209

Appendix B: Manton's Works: A Guide for Future
    Reading   217

Bibliography   223

About the Illustrations   229

Index of Subjects and Names   233

Index of Scripture   240

ILLUSTRATIONS

1.1   Portrait of Thomas Manton by Robert White   20

1.2   Picture of Wadham College, Oxford, where Manton attended college during the late 1630s   33

1.3   Portrait of King Charles I in 1648, who was taken prisoner during the English Civil War and beheaded for treason in 1649 by Parliament   37

2.1   Picture of Pride's Purge, when Gen. Pride "purged" many members of Parliament from their seats   45

2.2   Portrait of Edmund Calamy, one of the authors of *Smectymnuus,* as well as a very active member of the Westminster Assembly and personal friend to Manton   52

2.3   Picture inside Westminster Hall, where Charles I was tried and sentenced to death   54

3.1   Portrait of John Owen, a contemporary of Manton's who was a congregationalist   61

3.2   Picture of Charles II, whom Manton (and others) invited to return to become King of England in 1660   64

3.3   Portrait of William III, who became the King of England with his wife, Mary, in 1689   73

4.1   Portrait of Martin Luther by his friend Lucas Cranach   85

4.2   Portrait of John Calvin, the famous Protestant theologian of Geneva   90

5.1   Title page of Manton's Commentary   102

6.1   Map of Virginia in the seventeenth century, where the Teackles lived   122

6.2   Title page for Luther's *The Babylonian Captivity of the Church*, where he attacks the seven sacraments   127

6.3   Title page of the Authorized Version (KJV), which was used by countless theologians like Hammond   134

7.1   Portrait of Richard Baxter, a friend and colleague of Manton's   146

8.1   Portrait of Oliver Cromwell, who ruled England during the 1650s   169

9.1   Medal of Ulrich Zwingli, the first Reformer to preach verse-by-verse on Sundays, rather than following the liturgy   192

FOREWORD

For many Christians, the Puritans have become a staple of their everyday lives. It is perhaps strange that men who lived so many hundreds of years ago still speak with such power to a generation raised on video games, computers, cell phones, and, more recently, texting, iPods, and iPads. Their popularity, therefore, is clearly not rooted in their compatibility with the tools of modern life; rather, it lies in the seriousness of their devotion and the greatness of the themes they engage. Human sinfulness, God's grace, the glory of Christ, and the certainty of the life to come: these are all staples of Puritan literature, and they are of perennial interest to God's people in all places and at all times.

For all the renewed interest in the Puritans, many of them remain little known. The names of John Owen, Richard Baxter, and Thomas Watson are familiar to many, but a host of other figures of equal theological and pastoral acumen feature less frequently on reading lists. In part this is because of the complexity of their language. In an era of sound bites and tweets, the rolling, periodic sentences of the Puritans can make them difficult to read. It is also the result of the differences between their world and ours: for all the common themes noted above, there is still something alien about seventeenth-century England. It is not the world of the twenty-first century.

Thus, it is a great pleasure to introduce this book by Derek Cooper. Dr. Cooper has done the church a great service by writing a clear and helpful introduction to the works of a Puritan who is perhaps less well known today than some of his contemporaries and yet who modeled the ideal of a Puritan pastor in so many ways. Thomas Manton was the complete package: a careful exegete, a passionate preacher, a churchman, a pastor, a theologian, a shepherd of souls. As with many other seventeenth-century figures, his writings are voluminous, and aspiring readers need a good map and guidebook to help them make their way through the sometimes dense material. This is precisely what Dr. Cooper has provided.

This book, excellent as it is, should not be the end of the story; it is rather aimed at whetting the reader's appetite for Manton in particular and the Puritans in general. I have no doubt that it will do precisely that.

Carl R. Trueman
Westminster Theological Seminary, Pennsylvania
March 2011

ACKNOWLEDGMENTS

This book is the result of several years of research into the life and thought of Puritanism in general and Thomas Manton in particular. So when it comes to acknowledging those who have played an important role in the formation and completion of the book, it only makes sense to me to give thanks to Thomas Manton himself! Although he has been dead for more than 300 years, I am thankful that he lived, and I certainly hope that this book faithfully represents his life and legacy. One of the greatest acts of love we show for others is to remember them; so the task of writing this book is actually an exercise in obeying Jesus' command to love others.

Besides Manton himself, I would additionally like to thank Marvin Padgett and the staff at P&R. I appreciate Marvin's enthusiasm for the Puritans, his oversight of this project, and the friendliness of the P&R staff. Everyone in the process has been helpful and pleasant, and I am appreciative of their support. My gratitude also belongs to Brandon Withrow, who has been helpful in answering a host of questions on a variety of topics. My wife Barb always merits praise, and I am forever appreciative of her support of me and the work I do. In particular, I would like to thank Carl for writing the foreword to this book; I have learned a great deal about Puritanism from him. I am also thankful to Tim Wengert, who first let me explore the topics covered in this book and who provided needed insight. Many thanks go to John Pahl,

Eric Heen, Karl Krueger, Sam Logan, and Justin Gohl, who read over portions of this book at various stages and gave helpful feedback. Gratitude also belongs to William Baker and Jack Whytock for permission to use portions of "The Analogy of Faith in Puritan Exegesis" (*Stone-Campbell Journal* 12:2) and "Saving the Strawy Epistle" (*Haddington House Journal* 11:1) respectively. At Biblical Seminary, I would like to thank Lydia Putnam for her help in tirelessly securing many interlibrary loans as well as Kelly Pfleiger and Lucy Schantz for their help in scanning pages.

Finally, I would like to thank Steve Nichols. Steve's kind heart, support, flexibility, and eagerness to connect this book to P&R have been greatly appreciated, and it is to him that I dedicate this book. I hope this book only strengthens the Guided Tour series that he created and has sustained so well.

PART ONE

MANTON IN CONTEXT: A SEVENTEENTH-CENTURY ENGLISH PREACHER

The few who know him [today] would gladly testify, I am sure, that Thomas Manton was one of the best authors of his day.
—J. C. Ryle

Ministers who do not know Manton need not wonder if they are themselves unknown. —C. H. Spurgeon

In days like these, I am thankful that the publishers of Manton's *Works* have boldly come forward to offer some real literary gold to the reading public. I earnestly trust that they will meet with the success which they deserve.
—J. C. Ryle

I shall now come to speak . . . of Dr. Thomas Manton . . . a name worthy of precious and eternal memory.
—William Bates

Remembering Thomas Manton

Although there are a select few today, echoing William Bates's words above, who certainly hold the name of Thomas

Manton as "precious" in their sight, there are far more who regard this name as anything but an "eternal memory." Instead, it is a name that is completely forgotten. Notwithstanding his obscurity today, however, Thomas Manton was a noted preacher, author, and public figure in seventeenth-century England. He wrote hundreds of sermons or exegetical works in addition to penning the preface to the second edition of the Westminster Confession of Faith (1658). He participated in key discussions on political and religious issues and made several appearances before the English Parliament. What is more, as the rector of St. Paul's, Covent Garden, he pastored an important congregation that included many persons of note. In fact, not only did Manton serve as a personal chaplain to Lord Protector Oliver Cromwell, but he was also invited to be a personal chaplain to King Charles II due, in part, to his involvement on the committee to restore Charles II to the throne subsequent to Cromwell's death. From these years until his death in 1677, Thomas Manton was a prominent clergyman who was well known and well respected by conformists and nonconformists alike.

Despite his importance in matters political and religious, however, interest in Thomas Manton's life has been sparse. This is apparent at both the academic and popular levels. When it comes to the academic level, scholars have generally focused on Puritanism in general or isolated individuals such as John Owen or Richard Baxter in particular. Most references to Manton that interact at all with his life rely upon a very old work that is almost 150 years old—a memoir of Manton's life by Englishman William Harris. Originally written by Harris as an introduction to the first printing of Thomas Manton's complete works in 1870, this helpful yet dated biography represents the most exhaustive account of Manton's life in print.

When it comes to the popular level, awareness of Thomas Manton's life and writings are equally minimal. This is especially lamentable given that Manton's works were delivered and designed for the average Christian in the pew. As Luke Timothy Johnson rightly states about Manton in his commentary on James, "His work . . . is above all 'practical,' that is, directed to the religious life and practices of his learners; all his learning tends to this end." Unlike many of his more famous contemporaries, Manton's works were not scholarly treatises or academic tomes. Rather, they were "practical" biblical expositions and sermons, which he preached to his congregations for their spiritual edification, and only later published them at the invitation of those who wanted his powerful and pertinent sermons to be made available for others to read.

Speaking of these sermons, Manton's complete works contain more than 600 individual and collective sermons. Although this may not seem like many—given that Manton preached several days a week for thirty-five years—this is a great quantity compared to other notable Puritans. As Hughes Oliphant Old explains:

> [We] have a far richer selection of Manton's sermons than we have for any other leading Puritan preacher. Regrettably, Richard Baxter (1615–91) and Edmund Calamy (1600–1666), who are usually named with Manton as the three most prominent Puritan preachers, have not left us any appreciable collection of sermons. Manton, therefore, probably gives us the best sustained impression of Puritan preaching which is available.

Indeed, Manton illustrates Puritan preaching well, and it is therefore completely appropriate that a sustained look at his life and writings is finally in print.

Overview

In order to better familiarize ourselves with this largely forgotten Puritan pastor, we will take our guided tour of

Thomas Manton by looking at his life, writings, and legacy in three distinct parts. Each of the chapters in Part One focuses on different phases of Manton's life by narrating key events, by interacting with the historical circumstances of the day, and by engaging some of Manton's own writings that date from this time. Part Two concentrates on Manton's best-known work: his commentary on the book of James, which he preached week after week to his congregation outside of London. This section considers the similarities and differences between Manton's way of interpreting this letter in relation to the Protestant Reformers, Anglicans, and Puritans respectively. Finally, Part Three includes selections from Manton's works that are intended to introduce readers to some of his more noteworthy sermons and expositions. Collectively, this part focuses on Manton as citizen, pastor, and preacher. In addition to these three parts, two appendices discuss Manton's legacy as well as guide interested readers to his twenty-two-volume body of writings.

1

THE SERVITOR FROM SOMERSET, 1620–40

The seventeenth was the decisive century in English history.
Christopher Hill

I have come to know [Thomas Manton] so well that I could
pick him out from among a thousand divines if he were
again to put on his portly form, and display among modern
men that countenance wherein was "a great mixture of
majesty and meekness."
C. H. Spurgeon

Introduction: The Decisive Century

It is a commonly held view that the seventeenth century
was the most critical and crucial century in all of English
history. Even more specifically, authors like Christopher
Hill propose that the "decisive decades" of that century
"are those between 1640 and 1660." Hill's assessment of
the seventeenth century and these specific decades is certainly suggestive, as this period profoundly shaped British
history. Political tension between Parliament and Charles I
(1600–1649), economic hardships among the middle and

1.1. Portrait of Thomas Manton by Robert White.

lower classes, religious disputes within the Church of England, the outbreak of the English Civil War, the establishment of the Commonwealth and the Protectorate under Oliver Cromwell (1599–1658), as well as the restoration of the monarchy and the issuance of several key legislative acts all jointly suggest both the restlessness and the significance of this period in English history.

Thomas Manton lived during all of these events. His life stretched through more than half of the seventeenth century, and he was altogether active during the crucial decades between 1640 and 1660. Manton was born five years before the ascension of Charles I, and he died seven years before the death of Charles II (1630–85). The middle of his life was lived during the Commonwealth (1649–53) and the Protectorate (1653–59) under Oliver Cromwell (and briefly his son Richard), and he was one of three scribes who attended the Westminster Assembly (1643–49). Manton additionally served as one of several chaplains to Cromwell and preached on occasion before Parliament; later he resigned (by compulsion) under the Act of Uniformity in 1662 as the minister of his parish and was even imprisoned during the reign of Charles II. In all of these events, the changing rhythm and the restless activity of seventeenth-century England provide the decisive setting from which to understand the life and writings of Thomas Manton.

Despite Manton's position as one of the more active and important divines in this crucial period of English political and religious history, he has attracted little interest over the past 150 years. To correct this oversight, this chapter provides an overview of Manton's life and in the process demonstrates the important role that he played in that "decisive century" in England's history. Specifically, this chapter narrates the first half of Manton's life—from his birth to his graduation from Oxford and ordination within the Church of England—while the following two chapters in this section describe Manton's career during the middle and later years of his life.

Early Years: Childhood and Grammar School, 1620–35

Thomas Manton was born in the remote southwestern county of Somerset, England in 1620. As the parish minister (or rector) at that time, Manton's father, also named Thomas, baptized his son in March of that year at Lydeard St. Lawrence. By the time of his birth, Protestantism had existed in England for one hundred years. Both of Manton's grandfathers, in fact, were Protestant ministers in the Church of England, a lineage that explains in part why young Thomas entered the ministry. The other reasons why he entered the ministry were probably related to the economic advantage it afforded him (since he was of a lower social class) as well as his personal interest in and calling to the pastorate.

Little is known about Manton's early years and experiences. He attended his studies, notes William Harris, the English scholar and churchman of the nineteenth century who wrote a memoir of Manton's life, at "the free school of Tiverton" in Devonshire for several years. There Manton presumably encountered a very traditional curriculum of grammatical studies and Latin. His education was doubtlessly similar to his more famous contemporary John Owen's (1616–83), who while in grammar school in the 1620s studied grammar, literature, and, above all, Latin in preparation for future undergraduate studies at the University of Oxford.

In the early seventeenth century there were two such schools in the small town of Tiverton. The first is Blundell's School, which was founded upon the death of Peter Blundell in 1601. Interestingly, Bishop Joseph Hall (1574–1656), the clergyman who later ordained Manton, was offered the position of master upon the school's inception but declined. Samuel Butler subsequently accepted the position, and he would have been master during Manton's time there. The second free school in Tiverton in the early seventeenth century was Chilcott's. It was founded in 1609 upon the death of Robert Chilcott (Camyn), nephew to Peter Blundell. Little is known about the early history of this school.

It is difficult to determine precisely which of the two schools Manton attended. Records at Blundell's did not formally begin until 1770, and no extant records exist from Chilton's. However, there was arguably little difference between the two; both were intended to educate boys in the rudiments of learning that were required for admittance into the university. Manton's schooling was no doubt similar to Anthony Wood's description of his own at "a Latin school in a little house," since both Blundell's and Chilcott's would have been small at that time, and since they would have been supremely concerned with teaching their pupils Latin, the language of the academy.

Larger Religious and Political Events in England, 1620s–1630s

While young Thomas was studying Latin in a small school in the remote southwestern part of the country, England as a whole was experiencing great change. The long and stable rule of Elizabeth I (1558–1603) established peace and security in contrast to the previous years of unrest under the reigns of her half-siblings Edward (1547–53) and Mary (1553–58). Although the religious and political compromises that Elizabeth made in her reign helped stabilize the nation in many ways, they eventually created a rift that began to emerge after James I (1566–1625) became king at the queen's death in the opening years of the 1600s.

One of these rifts was the growing tension between different groups within the Church of England. On the one side were the episcopalians[1] (or proto-Anglicans), who preferred a more liturgical worship service as well as a church leadership model based on the authority of bishops. On the other side were the presbyterians (who, together with congregationalists and independents, became known as Puritans),[2] who preferred a more simple worship service and a church leadership model based on the authority of elders or "presbyters." In addition to these ecclesiological differences, there were, of course, additional theological and religious distinctions that separated these groups; but during the early part of the seventeenth century they were bent on staying united within the Church of England.

This unity gradually waned during James's reign (1603–25), but it was not until his son's tenure as King of England that this tension came to full force. Charles I, heir apparent to his father James I and grandson to Mary, Queen of Scots, inherited the English Crown in 1625. For a variety of reasons, Charles experienced great difficulty with Parliament throughout his reign, and he would eventually be brought up on charges of treason and executed in 1649 during the English Civil War. Unlike his father, who disagreed with many of the political and religious leaders and policies in England at the time but compromised when necessary, Charles was steadfast in his views. He made several ques-

1. The terms *episcopalian* and *presbyterian* in this book are lowercased since both refer to ministers in the Church of England. These two terms would refer to people from different denominations at a later point in history.

2. The use of the term *Puritans* here refers, in the words of Carl Trueman, "to those who wished to see a further reformation of worship in the Established Church in a direction which emphasized liturgical simplicity and the centrality of preaching. . . . Such Puritans were not separatists, however, as by and large, they remained within the church until expelled in 1662."

tionable decisions and appointments in his early years as king—including a very unpopular decision to marry a French Catholic princess at a time when Parliament was thoroughly Protestant and decidedly anti-Catholic, as well as making several appointments that further continued his uneasy relationship with Parliament.

One such religious and political appointment was Charles's decision to appoint William Laud (1573–1645) to the very important and influential bishopric of London in 1628. This was a striking blow to the Puritan cause, which was increasingly uneasy with the direction of the Church of England. For some time now, London had been a great stronghold of both Puritan and presbyterian ideas. The king's appointment of the Anglo-Catholic Laud caused great consternation, and it is at this time that Puritanism entered a new and more aggressive phase. This is because Laud—who was openly Arminian, strongly in favor of the episcopacy, highly ceremonial and sacramental, and generally opposed to the Puritans—began passing legislation that directly disfavored this group as well as nominating several bishops and others of note to higher positions in the church who were knowingly Arminian in theology. Laud's policies and actions at this time, though fully supported by King Charles I, caused mounting tensions that would only be resolved during the English Civil War and Restoration.

Adolescent Years: Oxford University, 1635–39

The king's appointment of people like William Laud to very influential positions affected many people, Thomas Manton included. Young Thomas's residence at Oxford actually coincided with that of Laud's who, as chancellor from 1630 to 1645, introduced several educational reforms at the university. Laud's chancellorship was heavily involved in the daily affairs of the school. It is believed, in fact, that Laud is largely responsible for the expansion of Arminianism within the university curriculum at Oxford, in much the same way that he was responsible for the changes in the church at large, which until this time had been largely Puritan and Calvinistic.

Manton entered Wadham College at Oxford University in March of 1635. Although Exeter College had been, notes Stephen Porter, "the most popular college for students from Somerset" for some time, Wadham became the "commonest destination" for students from the western counties in the early seventeenth century. Wadham was actually the newest addition to Oxford at this time. It was founded upon the death of Nicholas Wadham in 1610, and the new college was meticulously constructed through the efforts of Wadham's wife Dorothy for the next several years. Being founded by a descendant from a wealthy family rooted in the western part of the country, Wadham's new college naturally attracted students from that general area. According to the original statutes of Wadham, in fact, three scholars were to be admitted from Manton's home county of Somerset.

Manton matriculated to Wadham as a "servitor" or plebeian (the equivalent of a "sizar" at rival Cambridge University). This was the lowest of grades at Oxford, and it resonates with Stephen Porter's assertion that "Youths of lower social status went to the universities to obtain the training and qualifications required for them to develop a career, especially in the church." This was because a career in the church "was the single greatest outlet" or professional avenue for university students in the seventeenth century, especially for plebeians such as Manton. In line with the times, Manton was likely the first in his family of clerics to enter the university. The very opportunity to attend Oxford was either afforded by his being the only male child in the family or, what is perhaps more plausible, by receiving patronage by an aristocrat from his home area.

The economic factors to Manton's education are consonant with the development of the clerical profession in England during the seventeenth century. Unlike Manton's two grandfathers and his father, for instance, a university education became important for prospective clergymen only during the seventeenth century. Before then, most clergymen did not attend the university. By Manton's time, however, clerical education at the university level was on the rise. Historian Rosemary O'Day estimates, in fact, that about 15 percent of students at Oxford during the 1630s were "sons of clergy" who were probably following their fathers' footsteps into the ministry. In this way she wryly asserts that for plebeians such as Manton, "the degree was a meal-ticket."

It is in this context that Porter underscores the "economic" and "social" advantages received by plebeians such as Manton who attended the university. To do so as a servitor was certainly not ideal in such a class-conscious nation like England—where one's status upon birth largely determined one's status throughout one's life—but attending the university was a supreme opportunity for an increase in mobility and status. As a servitor, Manton would have waited upon the fellows in Wadham and received exemption from certain fees for room and board and lectures. Because of the "indignities and drudgery" that the rank of servitor entailed, Lawrence Stone argues that clergymen's sons often matriculated as "commoners or batteelers," which would have been a grade up the social ladder and therefore would have given the student greater social mobility and standing, rather than as servitors. Presumably due to economic necessity, however, Manton served as a servitor at Wadham.

During Manton's residency at Wadham College, Oxford was experiencing an explosion in its population at both the university and in the surrounding town—a reflection of the wider population growth throughout England. It is estimated that Oxford boasted a town population of 10,000 residents in the 1630s, while a third of the population lived at the university. This decade, interestingly enough notes Nicholas Tyacke, "saw the highest numbers of student admissions in any decade before the 1870s," coming to around 5,000 admissions in total, which eventually produced an influx of ministerial graduates in the middle of the seventeenth century. Despite the increase in admissions and population, however, the colleges rarely contained more than 200 students at a time. It is estimated that Wadham College, for example, housed around 100 members during Manton's residence. Hart Hall, where Manton spent his last days before graduating, was approximately the same size.

The Curriculum at Oxford, 1630s

The center of learning at Oxford (and Cambridge) in the seventeenth century was the undergraduate curriculum. This was so, historian Mordechai Feingold explains, because "it was shared by all students, irrespective of social background or length of stay." Every undergraduate ostensibly followed this course of study regardless of respective college, background, or future endeavor. In this respect, the undergraduate curriculum was "quintessentially humanistic"; it was designed to foster general familiarity with all subjects rather than specialization in any one in particular. Students were therefore exposed to a wide variety of subjects. A typical student, explains Feingold,

> ideally received grounding in the constituents of language, arts, and sciences, acquired the habits of reasoning and

judgement, and, perhaps most important, imbibed a love of literature that would last until one's dying day.

The aim of the undergraduate curriculum was therefore to instill in its students an appropriate disposition toward learning and a foundation upon which to build their own edifice of knowledge in the years subsequent to Oxford.

Similarly, as Cambridge historian William Costello explains in one of his books, logic was regarded at both Cambridge and Oxford as "the 'art of arts,'" the framework for all subsequent knowledge. He further characterizes the discipline as primarily Aristotelian, though Feingold attests the appropriateness of this categorization. What it was not, however, was Ramist. Feingold argues persuasively that Ramism waned in popularity within "two or three decades after [Peter] Ramus' death in 1572." There were many reasons why this occurred, not least, Feingold states, because the "movement as a whole scarcely retained intellectual respectability." Aristotelianism, by contrast, retained intellectual respectability for some time. And although the discipline of logic was not completely Aristotelian in the sense that students only studied Aristotle, Aristotelian logic was present in the curriculum; and it was certainly represented in the context of Oxford's emphasis on "the essential interconnectedness of knowledge," as well as in its attention to language and its construction.

Aristotle's interest in language and exact expression naturally coalesced with the sister art of logic, rhetoric. Renaissance sensitivity to rhetoric as exemplified in the works of, among others, Erasmus (1466–1536) had become the hallmark of a university education. However, rhetoric was not limited to modern authors; instead Feingold argues that it was "to be as comprehensive as possible, exercising the student in a variety of ancient and modern styles." In this way, it was very eclectic: Classic Greek and Latin writers such as Ovid, Virgil, Cicero, Horace, Seneca, and Petrarch featured heavily in the curriculum—as a cursory look at Manton's quotations from his sermons substantiates. In fact, Seneca and Petrarch were particular favorites of his, and it is natural to conclude that he learned to read and appreciate these authors while in grammar school and especially while at Wadham.

On the whole, there was a veritable "veneration of language" at Oxford during the Renaissance that contributed to its dominance in the curriculum. Feingold notes how William Laud's chancellorship further perpetuated this emphasis on language as the "ultimate purpose of both the BA and MA courses." Attention to eloquence naturally directed students to the Greek and Latin classics. The Oxford historian Charles Mallet asserts, for instance, that first-year students at Wadham were required to attend lectures "on Greek and Latin authors three times a week." The prevalence of Manton's frequent allusions to classic authors in his works reveals his indebtedness to his earlier education, particularly his exposure to Latin classics.

According to Oxford historian George Brodrick, undergraduates most likely attended lectures in grammar, rhetoric, ethics, logic, moral philosophy, and Greek; and most students took the Bachelor's degree at the end of their fourth year. The so-called Laudian Code of 1636 suggests that the lectures closely followed the medieval educational system: namely, the *trivium* ("the three roads"), which included grammar, logic, and rhetoric; and the more advanced *quadrivium* ("the four roads"), which included arithmetic, geometry, music, and astronomy. Specifically, Feingold states,

Rhetoric was prescribed for the first year, dialectic for the second and third years, and moral philosophy—along with

Greek and arithmetic—was studied by students in their third and fourth years.

The required examinations for the Bachelor of Arts at the completion of their studies tested students in the subjects of the lectures they attended. What is more, as Brodrick explains, "the method of interrogation seems to have been exclusively oral; and the authority of Aristotle was to be paramount within the whole sphere of his voluminous writings."

As a prospective minister, Manton would have certainly benefited from the public lectures he attended as well as the many disciplines he studied through the course of his undergraduate education. Especially valuable would have been what were called "declamations" and "disputations." Whereas the declamation was essentially a short speech that students gave in order to refine their speaking abilities as well as their literary and rhetorical insight, the disputations were debates between students that evaluated their abilities to think quickly and conduct arguments reasonably and eloquently. Manton would have engaged in several of these exercises during his undergraduate days in various subjects, and involvement in them would have greatly benefited him during his career, which focused so heavily on reasoning and speaking well.

Besides the lectures, the disputations, and the declamations, there was an additional resource at the university that would have been particularly influential in the course of Manton's education: the tutor. Tutors in the seventeenth century supervised the studies of their pupils and recommended specific books. By the end of the sixteenth century, and certainly by the time of Manton's matriculation at Wadham, all of the colleges at Oxford had mandated the appointing of tutors for all incoming students. Because tutors offered personal guidance to students as well as additional instruction to the formal lectures and disputations, a student's tutor was perhaps the most important person with whom the student would be in contact.

Unlike his more famous acquaintance John Owen, who studied at Queen's College, Oxford under Thomas Barlow (1607–91), it is not possible to determine who Manton's tutor was while at nearby Wadham College. The warden or head of Wadham at this time was Daniel Estcot, but he probably influenced Manton less extensively than his tutor. Due to the fact that tutors differed widely in their management of their pupils, it is not possible to establish the specific books to which Manton's tutor would have directed him. Manton's tutor certainly supervised his progress in Latin and Greek, and he would have offered additional instruction as needed. But further information about Manton's tutor and the influence he may have had upon him is not known. What is most likely is that there were multiple influences on Manton's education, in terms of teachers, teaching method, and books.

From Bachelor to Doctor

Manton graduated with a Bachelor of Arts in 1639. For some unknown reason, he transferred to Hart Hall (now Hertford College) during his last months of study and thus graduated from this society instead of Wadham. Transferring from one college to another was far from uncommon at Oxford, but the exact reason for Manton's departure from Wadham is obscure. The most sensible explanation for this transfer was financial. This was because "halls" were cheaper than "colleges," and it was a regular occurrence for students to transfer to halls from colleges as a result. Another explanation, one given by Anthony Wood (1632–95), who wrote a generation after Manton and described him as "a hotheaded person," insinuates that Manton's temper was the reason for his transference to Hart Hall toward the end of his studies. Regardless of the exact cause of his departure from Wadham, Manton resided at the college and received supervision there for practically the entirety of his undergraduate studies at Oxford. In this way, it remains of little consequence that Manton transferred at the end of his undergraduate program to Hart Hall.

Although Manton graduated in 1639 and thereby concluded his on-campus requirements at the university level for good, he did not terminate his studies. Over the course of his career, Manton received two more degrees at Oxford: the Bachelor of Divinity and the Doctor of Divinity. According to the Laudian statutes, the degree of Bachelor of Divinity required seven years beyond the Bachelor of Arts, while the Doctor of Divinity required eleven. However, the students were not required to remain in residence while

1.2. Picture of Wadham College, Oxford, where Manton attended college during the late 1630s.

completing these degrees. In accordance with these statutes, Manton became a Bachelor of Divinity at Wadham (not Hart Hall) on April 20, 1654. He was awarded this degree on the ground that "he is a person of known worth, and a constant preacher in London." Six years later on November 19, 1660, he received the Doctor of Divinity at the request of Charles II—the highest degree Oxford offered.

The earning of the Doctor of Divinity at this time was prestigious, and throughout his lifetime Manton was regarded as a very learned pastor. As Anglican Bishop J. C. Ryle (1816–1900) would later proclaim, Manton was "the prince among the [Puritan] divines." From the years during his undergraduate studies at Wadham to the ones subsequent to becoming a Doctor of Divinity two decades later, Manton amassed an extensive library, particularly of books relating to divinity or theology. At the time of his matriculation to Wadham, that college maintained a collection of some 2,000 books on divinity in its private library. The much larger and more famous Bodleian library at Oxford was likewise available to Manton (though it is possible that as a servitor he was not allowed entrance there).

Although it is not known exactly which books Manton read while at Oxford, it is evident in his many writings that he was conversant with both classic and modern authors, secular and Christian ones. And it can further be conjectured, based on contemporary records, which books were available in the middle of the seventeenth century and which were popular or prominent around Manton's lifetime, especially for Puritans. Because Thomas Barlow was a tutor at nearby Queen's College while Manton was a student at Wadham, it is not implausible to conclude that Barlow's *On the Study of Theology*, which listed the books that he prescribed for his students including John Owen, would have been quite familiar to Manton.

A cursory glance at Barlow's list of books is impressive, encompassing a wide range of theological and exegetical works with which Manton would have probably been at least generally familiar, if not much more so. Upon his death in 1691, Barlow bequeathed his massive volume of books, which included the titles that he recommended to his students, to Bodleian Library. Although Manton's library was not as extensive as Barlow's, it was certainly noteworthy. The library catalogue of these books, which were all sold at an auction in London immediately after Manton's death in order to sustain his wife and children, contains hundreds of volumes, which the auctioneer William Cooper divides into various categories: Greek and Latin works, commentaries, theology, philosophy, history, and divinity. This list confirms the many reports about Manton being a very learned pastor and preacher who spent countless hours in his study in preparation for his sermons.

Ordination and Pastorate, 1639–40

When Manton graduated from Oxford in 1639, he was a mere nineteen years old. Although William Harris argues that this was especially noteworthy at the time, it is not necessarily as unusual as it appears. Several factors determined when students would matriculate to the university, not least of which was mastery of Latin. Therefore, there was a range of several years for incoming and graduating students. John Owen, for instance, graduated BA when he was sixteen years old, while his more famous pupil John Locke graduated BA when he was twenty-three. Rosemary O'Day estimates that the average age for incoming students was around seventeen years of age, but the age depended ultimately upon the mastery of Latin.

Shortly after his graduation from Oxford, Manton was ordained to the diaconate in the Church of England in 1640.

There is disagreement as to whether he ever received further ordination from the lower office of "deacon" to the higher one of "priest" at some point later in his career. Anthony Wood, for his purposes, reports that Manton was ordained to the priesthood in 1660 at Westminster Abbey. However, Harris's memoir of Manton, dating back to the second part of the nineteenth century, argues instead that Manton took orders as a deacon (and never as a priest) in the conviction that he had been "properly ordained to the ministerial office." This mind-set is based on the conviction that God is the one who officially ordains, so the human level of ordination—whether as a deacon or priest—is not as important. Harris bases this statement on the words of Edmund Calamy (1600–1666), a friend of Manton's. Given that Wood argues that Manton's ordination in 1660 was his only ordination within the Church of England, it is most likely not correct.

What appears most likely is that Manton was ordained to the diaconate in 1640 at the age of nineteen, but it is not possible to determine whether he was ever officially ordained to the priesthood later in his career. His appointment to the noteworthy rectorate at Covent Garden in London several years later could suggest that he was, but this is not definitive. What is more established is the record that it was the well-known author and bishop Joseph Hall who ordained Manton. Hall, the noted proponent of episcopalianism (Anglican episcopacy) and a satirist during the seventeenth century, was appointed to the bishopric of Exeter in 1627, an office that he held until he transferred to the see at Norwich in 1641. Because Hall was the bishop in the diocese to which Manton accepted his initial position in nearby Sowton, it was he who ordained young Thomas. In the ceremony Hall stated that Manton "would prove [to be] an extraordinary person" throughout his career, but little is known about the direct relationship between the two.

Manton in Relation to Changing Times

While Manton was graduating from the university and undergoing ordination in 1639–40, momentous changes were taking place in the country. The English Crown, under Charles I, was in the middle of an intense dispute with Scotland, which was known as the Bishop's War. Charles's

CHARLES I.

1.3. Portrait of King Charles I in 1648, who was taken prisoner during the English Civil War and beheaded for treason in 1649 by Parliament.

attempt to force the episcopacy upon the presbyterian Scots had been fiercely resented, and Charles was in a precarious position since he was in desperate need of money and support, but lacked both since he had refused to call Parliament in session for a decade and had attempted to rule the nation independently. Stubborn, but with no other options, Charles ordered the so-called Short Parliament into session in the spring of 1640 to help his situation, but the members offered no support for the king; so he hurriedly dissolved the Parliament only to have to convene the so-called Long Parliament a few months later once his situation was dire. The convening of the Long Parliament in the fall of 1640 was the beginning of the end of Charles's reign. Parliament, bitter over the king's failure to redress previous grievances and discontent with the economic, political, and religious direction in which Charles was leading the nation, effectively took control of the government. The series of events that ensued eventually erupted into a veritable war involving the three kingdoms of England, Scotland, and Ireland.

As all of these momentous events were transpiring, young Thomas Manton was embarking on the beginning of his career. His entire life, in fact, would be supremely interrelated with these events. Within just a few years, he would be forced to move his family out of harm's way on more than one occasion, and his eventual arrival in London during the Commonwealth would place him in a very advantageous position, only to be pushed out of prominence once the tide had turned in the opposite direction. In all of these events within this "decisive century," Manton was very much a man of his times, attempting to be faithful to his call to the pastorate in the midst of difficult and unprecedented circumstances.

2

THE LONDON PRESBYTERIAN, 1640‒56

Perhaps few men of the age in which [Thomas Manton]
lived had more virtues and fewer failings.
William Harris

Some people love to live in the fire and to handle the red-hot
questions of the age with passion and acrimony; but, alas,
this does no good.
Thomas Manton

Lecturer at Sowton, 1640–43

Opportunities for men with a Bachelor of Arts degree
with Manton's background were surprisingly limited in the
middle of the seventeenth century. This was due to the
dramatic increase in student admissions during the decade
of Manton's residence at Oxford, which had produced an
influx of university graduates in search of ministerial positions. Opportunities were thus scarce, since the ideal profession for many graduates was one in the ministry. As Stanley
Porter explains:

Youths of lower social status went to the universities to obtain the training and qualifications for them to develop a career, especially in the church. A university education provided them with opportunities which they could not otherwise have had. It also offered the widening of social horizons and increased geographical mobility. Although the levels of remuneration for teachers and the clergy in particular varied enormously the rewards to which a university entrant from a plebeian background aspired were partly economic. They were also social, for entry into the clergy endowed an individual with a status and respect in society which could only have been achieved with difficulty in another sphere.

This encapsulates Manton's situation, as the ministry afforded him the financial means necessary to progress economically as well as to gain important contacts that he would make use of throughout his lifetime, especially around London.

The ideal for an Anglican clergyman of Manton's background was to acquire a benefice or "living" within an established parish. This is because the holder of a living was entitled to the income that came from tithes through the parish. This ensured social and economic security as well as political influence. Until such a prime opportunity arose, however, other positions had to suffice. There were essentially three options. The first option for someone of Manton's training upon graduation would be continued residence at Oxford or Cambridge as a Master of Arts candidate and fellow at a college. This was the common path of many of Manton's contemporaries, such as John Owen who studied for this degree immediately after earning his Bachelor of Arts. The second option would be to teach at a grammar school as a principal or master, like Richard Baxter (1615–91) did for a couple of years between his ordination to the ministry and his establishment as the pastor at Kidderminster. Finally, the third option for recent graduates who intended to enter ministry was to be a kind of freelance clergyman by serving in a church on a part- or full-time basis. Manton pursued the latter option and never took the well-established path of earning a Master of Arts degree.

Manton's first position after graduating from Oxford appears to be as a lecturer in Sowton. At this time Sowton was a tiny village located in East Devon. It was a few miles away from the more important city of Exeter, where Bishop Hall resided, which was a dangerous place to be in the early 1640s due to the English Civil War. It was at Sowton that Manton preached his very first sermon, which was based on Jesus' command in the Sermon on the Mount, "Judge not, that you be not judged" (Matthew 7:1). It was also the place where he married Mary Morgan of Sidbury, Devonshire toward the end of his residence there, on May 15, 1643.

In Sowton, Manton held the position of lecturer from 1640 to 1643. At this time in the Church of England there was a variety of ways to refer to pastors. Three of the most common—curate, vicar, and rector—were distinguished by the manner in which they received their income. Whereas a curate generally received a small salary and a vicar received one portion of a parish's tithes, a rector received two portions of a parish's tithe and was therefore provided with a more stable income. As a young man ordained to the diaconate in the church, especially given the influx of recent graduates who were flooding the market, Manton had to work his way up the church ladder by taking less established and lower-paying positions as well as by residing in more remote areas until he was called to the rectorate in the London area several years later. This characterizes well his status at Sowton. His position as a "lecturer" was essentially equivalent to that of an assistant curate, which meant that it was temporary and did not pay well.

The Long Parliament, the English Civil War, and Colyton, Early 1640s

For the next several years, Manton and his wife Mary moved on several occasions. There were primarily two reasons for this. The first was that Manton's reputation as a gifted preacher, coupled with his zeal for presbyterianism (which he believed was both faithful to the Bible and helpful to the nation at large), would compel him to advance to more notable positions—specifically to the London area. By all accounts, Manton was a powerful preacher with much promise. As contemporary diarist Ralph Thoresby (1658–1724) wrote, for instance, Manton was heralded as "the king of preachers."

The second reason why the Mantons moved around so much was due to the fact that the English Civil War was just underway, as it roughly paralleled the beginning of Manton's professional career. The English Civil War was a series of conflicts and battles from 1642 to 1651 that involved England, Scotland, and Ireland. There were generally three stages to this war, beginning in 1642, but the causes of it stemmed from multiple economic, social, political, and religious factors.

By the early 1640s, bitterness and distrust between Parliament and King Charles I were widely apparent. Due to the king's refusal to convene Parliament for eleven years, the Long Parliament, which assembled in the fall of 1640 (just months after the Short Parliament was called but quickly dissolved), immediately began passing legislation that demonstrated its own authority as independent of—and in many cases superior to—the king's power. In the fall of 1641, Parliament passed the Grand Remonstrance, which commanded the king to answer to more than 200 grievances that Parliament had with the direction of the country. Within a few months Charles had realized the magnitude of the situation and fled with his family from his palace in the London area to Oxford, where those loyal to him congregated.

With the king gone, the Long Parliament effectively took control of the government and began assembling its own army. Known as parliamentarians or "roundheads" (due to the shortness of their hair in contrast to their more high-class opponents), those in line with this assembly began a series of armed conflicts with the royalists or "cavaliers" (due to their long hair and flamboyant clothing and attitude), those who were loyal to the king. The cause of the disagreement and battle, at this time at least, was not about whether there should be a democratic government or a monarchy; rather, the disagreement was more about whether there should be a constitutional monarchy (parliamentarians) or whether there should be a monarchy based on the divine right of monarchs or absolute power (royalists).

Within just a couple of years of Manton's graduation from the university, the king and those members of Parliament who were royalists convened at Oxford as the base of operations against the parliamentarians, who were at Westminster. The first phase of the war (1642–46) resulted in victory for the parliamentarians. The king was taken prisoner by a Scottish army and handed over to the parliamentarians, who imprisoned him. The second phase of the war (1648–49) was instigated by the king who, though still in captivity (even though he had escaped and had been moved around), was plotting with rival factions. Specifically, he persuaded the Scots to invade England— under the promise that he would allow presbyterianism rather than episcopacy in Scotland—and he rallied many of the royalists to attack several key areas; but the parliamentarians were quick to defeat these uprisings. As Charles languished in prison, the Long Parliament debated whether (and how) to reinstate the king to the monarchy.

It was at this time that one of the more remarkable events in English history occurred. In December of 1648, General Pride, who was a commander in the New Model Army, marched upon Parliament and effectively "purged" many of its members from entering the assembly. The New Model Army, which the Long Parliament had instituted in 1645 to battle against the royalists, had gradually become impatient with the Long Parliament's willingness to countenance the king, given all that he had done over the past several years, as well as Parliament's slowness to pay the soldiers their money and provide for their welfare. Although it could be stated that both the New Model Army and the Long Parliament were composed largely of Puritans, the former consisted mostly of independents (who wanted more political and religious autonomy), while the later consisted mostly of presbyterians (who were more politically and religiously moderate and in favor of the monarchy). In this way, it is manifest how the term *Puritan* can encompass any number of individuals or groups who may disagree on a whole host of religious, political, and economic issues.

The culmination of this growing tension between the Long Parliament and the New Model Army was known as "Pride's Purge." In all, almost 200 Parliamentary members (MPs) were purged or barred from entering the assembly by General Pride, and those who were allowed entrance were given orders to set up a high court that would try Charles I. The remaining MPs, consisting of what is now regarded as the Rump Parliament, soon convened and eventually found the king guilty of being a "tyrant, traitor, murderer, and public enemy," for which cause he was beheaded in January of 1649. It was also at this time that the Rump Parliament abolished both the House of Lords and the

2.1. Picture of Pride's Purge, when Gen. Pride "purged" many members of Parliament from their seats.

monarchy. It goes without saying that this action was unprecedented at this time in history and that it completely divided the country.

The magnitude of these historic events did not leave Manton (and the nation at large) unaffected. Besides being forced to move around, Manton would be at the discretion of the changing authority structures while in London, whether positive to him (in the beginning) or negative to him (toward the middle and end of his career). After around three years as lecturer or assistant curate at Sowton, Manton was forced to move to the eastern town of Colyton, Devonshire at the end of 1643. This town offered Manton and his family better protection than the immediate area of Exeter provided, which the royalists had besieged in September of 1643.

Colyton further offered Manton the opportunity to offer weekly lectures that were well-attended. Manton's residence at Colyton was brief, and there remains only a modicum of information about him during this time. What is known is that the area in the southwest was increasingly perilous due to the Civil War, and the royalist advances in this general area against the parliamentarians compelled Manton to flee the west altogether, which he did in the summer of 1645 when he moved to London. There he would ultimately spend the rest of his life.

London: Presbyterianism and the Westminster Assembly, 1643–49

Times were difficult in London during the 1640s, but it offered better protection and opportunity for a presbyterian like Manton. In 1643, for example, Parliament passed an act that effectively abolished the episcopacy; later that year the body convened the Westminster Assembly to advise it on matters relating to church government. Finally, Parliament's execution of Archbishop William Laud two years later (1645) seriously threatened the cause and certainly the security of Charles I, who was, as noted above, eventually beheaded in 1649.

Despite several previously unsuccessful attempts of the Puritans in the House of Commons to convene an assembly that would attempt to make changes in the religious structures (for the simple reason that Charles I had refused to sign the acts into law), the Long Parliament was finally able to convene what is known as the Westminster Assembly in 1643—without the king's authority. The assembly met regularly until 1649. At any given time, the assembly consisted of less than eighty people (the vast majority of whom were divines or pastors and theologians), being composed mostly of presbyterians and independents. Among these two groups of Puritans, the presbyterians sought to remain within the Church of England but to push for a presbyterian form of church government; while the independents or congregationalists sought congregational autonomy and, eventually, independence from the state church. The assembly held more than 1,000 sessions over the course of its six years and produced several documents. Despite the assembly's lengthy and protracted work, however, none of its decisions or decrees endured after the Restoration in 1660, except in Scotland.

The tone of the Westminster Assembly was conservative. The members initially attempted to rework the Thirty-Nine Articles of Religion—the guiding confession of the Church of England—but eventually abandoned this project as it united with the Scottish Covenanters, who were an important group of Scots who advocated presbyterianism and opposed the rising of episcopalianism under the reign of Charles I. The reason for this union between the English and Scottish was pragmatic in nature. Because Irish Catholics threatened to join with the (English) royalists, the Long Parliament decided to unify with the Scottish Covenanters in order to fight off those loyal to the king.

This agreement, called the Solemn League and Covenant (1643), required, on the one hand, that the Scots would help the Long Parliament against the royalists, while, on the other, that the Westminster Assembly would agree to rework the theology and polity of the Church of England in a more reformed and presbyterian direction. Over the next several years, the assembly produced a series of religious documents that did just that. The Directory for the Public Worship of God, The Form of Presbyterial Church Government, as well as the Westminster Confession of Faith and the Shorter and Larger Catechisms all established a new course for the Church of England; but its attempts to replace the Thirty-Nine Articles of Religion and the Book of Common Prayer with these documents was short-lived.

Manton at St. Mary's, Stoke Newington, 1645–56

Thomas Manton moved to the vicinity of London right in the middle of these turbulent events. As the Westminster Assembly illustrates, London by this time was a popular destination for Puritans and presbyterians like Manton, and parliamentarian Colonel Alexander Popham's (1605–69) nomination and patronage of the young pastor to the living at Stoke Newington is not surprising given Manton's theological positions. (Popham was also patron of a much better-known man from Somerset, John Locke. Apparently Popham had commanded Locke's father during the Civil War, and he served as patron to young John through his years at Westminster and Christ's Church, Oxford, under the deanship of John Owen.)

At this time in England's history, Stoke Newington was still a tiny village immediately north of London in Middlesex. An opening had become available at the church there, which was named St. Mary's, upon the sequestration of William Heath, whose royalist leanings found little support as the parish became increasingly parliamentarian during the Civil War. In contrast to Heath, the parish endeavored to find a rector who would conform to its cause, and to this end Popham nominated Manton in 1644. Manton therefore relocated to Stoke Newington in the summer of July 1645 where he soon became a very respected and acknowledged leader of the presbyterians in the London area. His popularity and leadership skills would both be very important to his career in London.

Manton's career at Stoke Newington was a hectic one despite the great success he experienced. It was this way in part as a result of the political and religious disturbances that the Civil War had caused. Although Manton was never directly involved with any of the fighting, nor did he travel with Cromwell as a chaplain as John Owen had done, he was involved in other causes. One of these was the attempt to establish presbyterianism in the London area. This attempt naturally coalesced with the design of the Westminster Assembly, which, as mentioned above, had been convened in London right before Manton's appointment to the living at Stoke Newington. By the time of the Assembly's convocation in the summer of 1643, Manton was a mere twenty-three years old and not well known outside of London; so he was not nominated as one of the original divines. However, he did become one of three scribes at the assembly over the course of its many sessions, and he wrote a preface to the second edition of the Westminster Confession of Faith in 1658.

Manton's participation in the Westminster Assembly, as well as his other activities around London while he was rector at Stoke Newington, indicates his growing prominence during the 1640s and 1650s. Having earned the reputation of being an acknowledged leader of presbyterians in London, he regularly made appearances before Parliament as a preacher. In fact, it appears that Manton was called to preach before the Long Parliament on at least six occasions, beginning in the summer of 1647.

Manton's first sermon preached at Parliament was entitled "Meat out of the Eater; or, Hopes of Unity in and by Divided and Distracted Times," which was based on Zechariah 14:9. In the doctrinal section of this sermon Manton explains:

> Differences in religion stir up the greatest violences and most deadly hatred; that which should restrain and bridle our passions is the fuel of them. As long as there is difference in religion and worship there will be disturbances, and there cannot be that quiet and happy security which the promises do generally annex to those times.

In contrast to the present times of disunity, Manton adds that "in the latter days there shall be great unity in the church of God," and as such it should be England's aim to welcome those days and participate in them. Specifically, England's participation in that day, according to Manton, would occur by establishing presbyterianism as the official church system in England, in contrast to the "corruptions of episcopacy," and by allowing only minor accommodation for dissenting opinions. For Manton, the disorder of the nation could only be rectified by the nation's turning collectively to God and by the state and church working together toward that end.

Exactly a year later Manton preached again before Parliament in a fast sermon on Revelation 3:20, which he entitled "England's Spiritual Languishing; with the Causes and the Cure." In the sermon Manton lamented the current state of "English Christians" and called for a renewed godliness in the hearts and minds of those in England who desired to remain faithful to Christ until he returns. Once more Manton's plea in the sermon was for the Long Parliament to settle presbyterianism as a means to unite the country and to repair the damage that had taken place. Indeed, in each of these sermons preached at Parliament—which, as was customary, was printed during Manton's lifetime—he clearly indicated his presbyterian leanings. He, along with many others, believed that the institution of presbyterianism in London, and thus all of England, was the only sure cure for the "disease" of disorder and religious deterioration during the calamitous times in England's history.

It is for this reason that Manton published *Smectymnuus Redivivus* in 1653—a republication of the original document called *Smectymnuus*. This document, which was initially written in 1641 by Stephen Marshall, Edmund Calamy, Thomas Young, Matthew Newcomen, and William Spurstowe, was so called based on an acronym consisting of the initials of each of the authors above. The document was written in response to Bishop Joseph Hall's impassioned defense of episcopalianism in *A Humble Remonstrance* published a year before. Hall, who found himself in a delicate position later in his career, was both anti-Laudian and, in the present case, anti-presbyterian. In contrast to Hall's position, who, it should be recalled, ordained Manton, the latter argued in his preface that

> if the quarrel of episcopacy were once cleared, and brought to an [end], we should not be so much in the dark in other areas of discipline, [since] the conviction of an error on solid grounds being the best way to find out the truth.

The issue was simple for Manton: presbyterianism was the best way to organize the church and unify the nation.

To the dismay of presbyterians like Manton, however, Parliament did not establish presbyterianism in any substantial way. Efforts were made around London, but even there the presbyterian system of governance was short-lived. Manton himself was involved in the classis movement in London, which attempted to organize local churches according to the presbyterian model, but this was largely unsuccessful. Presbyterians like Manton were also dismayed at the palpable disconnect between the army and Parliament. Pride's Purge and the Rump Parliament's execution of Charles I frustrated the objectives of the presbyterians since they sought a negotiated settlement with

2.2. Portrait of Edmund Calamy, one of the authors of *Smectymnuus*, as well as a very active member of the Westminster Assembly and personal friend to Manton.

Charles I. After the execution of the king, their party was in a precarious position.

This description of presbyterians at this time in English history characterizes well Manton's own religious and political views. He utterly disapproved of Charles I's execution, and he would consequently become part of the discussions in Breda, Holland to entreat the king's son (Charles II) to return a decade later. As a presbyterian, Manton advocated the reestablishment of the monarchy. In fact, Manton, along with other presbyterians such as Edmund Calamy, signed a treaty that vindicated themselves from Charles I's death, and Manton was further acquainted with many who even conspired against the regime of those who killed the king for the return of Charles II.

The document these conspirers produced in 1649 was called *An Apologeticall Declaration*, which should not be confused with the *Apologetical Narration* (1644)—a document produced by independents in the Westminster Assembly who were discontent with the presbyterians, who were the dominant group in the assembly. The former document (1649) condemned how "an arbitrary and illegal power" had usurped its authority by executing the king. The result of this document was the arrest, trial, and execution of Christopher Love (b. 1618) in the summer of 1651. Love, along with many others, had corresponded with Charles I's wife on the Continent as well as with their son and heir to the throne, Charles II. Although Love was not the only one involved in these discussions to reinstate the monarchy, Oliver Cromwell desired to make an example out of him in order to keep the presbyterians from attempting future correspondence with Charles II, who by this time was in the process of amassing Scottish and English support to defeat Cromwell. Manton, for his part, risked his own life to preach Love's funeral sermon. The following year this

2.3. Picture inside Westminster Hall, where Charles I was tried and sentenced to death.

sermon, along with many of Love's own sermons, was published. In the sermon Manton concludes by stating that "memory is not abolished in heaven, but perfected"; as such, instead of commending Love's life, he admonishes Love's congregation at St. Lawrence Jewry to continue his legacy. The thrust of the sermon, however, was subtly directed against the English government for partaking in this travesty. Manton managed to walk a fine line between supporting his friend and criticizing the king.

Manton's Sermons at Stoke Newington

Besides establishing presbyterianism and preaching before Parliament, Manton was also engaged in many other activities while rector at Stoke Newington. In fact, perhaps the most important feature of his ministry at Stoke Newington relates to his expositions of Scripture. Being part of a tradition that stretched as far back as Ulrich Zwingli (1484–1531) and John Calvin (1509–64), who preached through entire biblical books rather than following a lectionary, Manton participated in a well-known Puritan practice of preaching continuously through Scripture.

Especially noteworthy are his sermons or "practical commentaries" on Isaiah 53, James, and Jude. These expositions are significant for three reasons. First, in contrast to the regular sermons that Manton preached twice on Sundays, Manton composed these expositions of Scripture and delivered them as weekday lectures. These expositions offered Manton the opportunity to exposit Scripture in a more systematic and continuous manner than would otherwise be possible for a typical Anglican liturgy on Sundays. They additionally afforded him the opportunity to expound texts of his choosing—texts that were no doubt relevant to the times. His preface to his commentary on Jude, for instance, begins with a description of the two great enemies of the church, "persecutors and sectaries," and he dedicates the remainder of his exposition to developing this theme.

Second, Manton's expositions of James and Jude while at Stoke Newington represent his only two complete biblical expositions. Although Manton preferred to teach and preach through specific sections of the Bible instead of isolated verses, he never composed a complete biblical commentary aside from those on James and Jude. This is somewhat surprising given Manton's interest in expounding Scripture and his fondness for working with continuous passages. The absence of additional commentaries on Scripture, however, is probably more pragmatic than intentional. As the years passed and his popularity and renown increased, Manton became more involved in the practical affairs of the church—especially during the 1650s and 1660s. Manton's ejection from the pulpit in 1662 and the hardships he endured afterward doubtlessly deterred him further from the consuming task of writing biblical commentaries, since he really had no venue from which to preach. As will be discussed in the following chapter, Manton was intimately involved in many political and religious discussions in the course of the Civil War and the Restoration. These gatherings would have required a great deal of his time.

Last, the expositions of Scripture that Manton composed while at Stoke Newington remain significant because they represent his earliest ventures at expounding the biblical text. It is striking and certainly a testimony to his intellectual and spiritual character that he researched, wrote, and delivered practically each of these expositions before the age of thirty. The chronological order of these three "practical commentaries" is Isaiah 53, James, and Jude, all coinciding sequentially with his rectory at Stoke Newington. The exposition of Isaiah 53 remains the most difficult to date precisely, but it most likely was the first one composed—perhaps in the middle of the 1640s.

Manton wrote his most famous commentary on the book of James toward the end of the 1640s, and it went through three printings: 1651, 1652, and 1657. He lectured on the letter four days a week while he was rector of Stoke Newington. And, in the words of William Harris, this commentary illustrates Manton's greatest exposition, as it

> has been thought by good judges to be one of the best models of expounding Scripture, and to have joined together with the greatest judgments the critical explication and practical observations upon the several parts.

Manton expounded the book of Jude immediately after James, and Harris notes that this commentary "was almost finished while he continued at Newington." He most likely completed it in the late 1640s and prepared it for publication in 1651, with subsequent printings following.

Conclusion: Manton's Sensitivity to England's Unrest

As mentioned throughout this chapter, England was in the midst of great disorder and restlessness while Manton was preparing and preaching his sermons. The fragility of the English nation naturally impacted Manton's career as a minister in the Church of England. This is especially the case for a clergyman in the London area who was becoming so well regarded among the nobility and people of means. Manton, for his part, dealt with the problems in England in the most effective way he could: instead of entering the political arena or joining the army, he spoke through the pulpit. Manton spiritually indicted the English nation and suggested repair of the social unrest by means of moral reform. He did this, as discussed above, in three ways: first, through his sermons at Parliament; second, through his continued leadership in the classis movement to establish presbyterianism; and third, through his sermons and lectures to his congregation at Stoke Newington.

To address pubic concerns by means of a lecture or commentary was potentially difficult for a Reformed pastor such as Manton. This is due to the established exegetical practices of Reformed commentators in the line of William Perkins (1558–1602) and John Calvin, whose primary concern when preaching or lecturing was expounding the intention of the author—not necessarily interacting with the events of the day. The reticence on the part of Reformed exegetes to step outside the biblical text determines in part why Manton dealt with social issues only indirectly. It would be wrong to conclude, however, that Manton was not interested in addressing national concerns. He certainly was. But as a Reformed biblical commentator, he dealt with national issues only when, in his view, the text of this or that biblical section lent itself legitimately to such issues. And, based on the sermons he delivered to his congregation as well as to the greater public, it is quite clear that Manton did not turn a blind eye to the great and momentous changes that were taking place in England. On the contrary, he addressed them in the best way he could by the means that were afforded him as a presbyterian pastor in London within the Church of England.

3

The King of Preachers, 1656–77

Forenoon at home; after, walked to Newington to see the
church, and the eminent Dr. Manton's funeral, who, being
deservedly styled the King of Preachers, was attended by the
vastest number of ministers of all persuasions that ever I saw
together in my life.

Ralph Thoresby

He was no fomenter of faction, but studious of the public
tranquillity. He knew what a blessing peace is, and wisely
foresaw the pernicious consequences that attend divisions.

William Bates

Manton the Preacher, 1656–62

Thomas Manton became rector of St. Paul's, Covent
Garden in 1656. Lord Protector Oliver Cromwell was by
now very much in power, and in the summer of that year
he was making preparations for battle against Spain.
Within a couple of years he would be dead, and his son
Richard's pitiable reign paved the way for Charles II's
eventual return as king. Despite Manton's mild refusal
to cooperate with the republic's government and his desire

for the reinstitution of the monarchy, he fared well during the Commonwealth.

During much of the 1650s, in fact, he was appointed to several respectable tasks. In 1654 he was appointed as one of several triers or commissioners within the Church of England, which enabled him to evaluate men's calling to the ministry. Manton was one of thirty-eight commissioners chosen, but he was only one of a handful of presbyterians commissioned to the task; the others were congregationalists like Thomas Goodwin and John Owen. Because of his conciliatory disposition, Manton was also called to participate in many other activities. For example, he participated in discussions among congregationalists, the Church of Scotland, and, on issues of religious toleration, Richard Baxter; he was a lecturer at Westminster Abbey and a chaplain to Cromwell; and he even sat on a council to hear proposals for the readmission of the Jews into England. In all these activities, Manton earned a reputation for being a moderate and cooperative man of strong character. This correlates with what he preached to his congregation: "Be zealous, and yet with temperateness and moderation."

It is in part for this reason that Manton was chosen to become the new rector at Covent Garden subsequent to the resignation of Obadiah Sedgwick. St. Paul's, Covent Garden, was actually a very recent parish, completed only in the 1630s. The patron of the parish was William Russell, Earl (and later Duke) of Bedford, and the building, which was seen as very contemporary at this time, was designed by Inigo Jones at a price of around £5,000. Apparently the London feoffees (or trustees) had initially intended to purchase this cathedral from the Earl of Bedford in order to channel through it their own style of preacher and lecturer, but William Laud eventually stymied their efforts.

Because of its patron, its prime location in London, and Manton's excellent preaching, St. Paul's attracted several important people, especially of the nobility. Important individuals included Oliver St. John, MP; John Evelyn, diarist and a founding member of the Royal Society (1660); Sir William Fleetwood; and Archbishop James Usher, who resided at Covent Garden and preached at the church occasionally before his death in the same year that Manton was appointed as rector. Although Manton endeavored to establish presbyterianism at St. Paul's as he had done at Stoke Newington, the parishioners

3.1. Portrait of John Owen, a contemporary of Manton's who was a congregationalist.

resisted this; and, for his part, Manton cooperated. This resistance to presbyterianism came to a head toward the end of his ministry there as a result of years of his refusal to read the liturgy. Ultimately his congregation, clearly a foreshadowing of the resurgent Anglicanism arising in England upon the restoration of Charles II, "petitioned the bishop of London," writes Francis Bremer, "in January of 1661 to force Thomas Manton to use the Prayer Book service," to which he conformed.

The tendency of many parishes then to resist presbyterianism coincides approximately with the end of the Commonwealth and the hastening of the Restoration. Oliver Cromwell, who had risen to power during the English Civil War, had effectively taken control of England (and Scotland) in 1649, but his untimely death in 1658 did not bode well for the continuation of the Commonwealth. The next two years after his death produced uncertainty and unrest, as his son Richard was unable to maintain the authority of his father. Although Manton and other presbyterians tolerated Richard, who only ruled for less than six months, under the conviction that he would further their cause and restore religious unity, Richard's brief tenure as Protector made this impossible.

In the beginning of 1660, General George Monck marched on London and effectively restored the Long Parliament by reinstating those members, mostly presbyterians, who had been excluded by Pride's Purge twelve years previously. Monck was forced to do this after he found the Rump Parliament unwilling to dissolve itself and sit for new elections. This reconstituted Long Parliament agreed to dissolve itself in the spring of 1660, and a new Parliament was convened in the summer. The reconstituted Long Parliament additionally dispatched several noteworthy and moderate presbyterians such as Edmund Calamy and Thomas Manton to Holland to negotiate with Charles II. By now it was apparent that

England's attempt at self-government without the monarchy had failed, and the nation was ready for stability and peace.

The newly convened Parliament, known as the Convention Parliament, was composed mostly of royalists. Their first order of business was to reinstate the monarchy. The goal of Manton and others who entered into negotiations with Charles II in Breda was, in the words of Michael Watts, "comprehension in the new religious establishment." Despite major setbacks and quarrels, it was Manton's desire for the Church of England to be one. He, as Peter Toon explains, "still held [to] the final ideal of the one Church containing all the Protestant Christians and ministers in the nation." On the basis of Charles II's words in 1660, such a sentiment was not wholly unrealistic. As Richard Baxter writes in his autobiography, Charles II's "promises of peace" encouraged Manton and others "to high expectations." These expectations were raised on the basis of Charles's *Declaration of Breda* and were the terms of Charles II's acceptance of the crown, in response to General Monck's invitation. The document stated that

> no man shall be disquieted or called in question for differences of opinion in matter of religion which do not disturb the peace of the kingdom.

To be sure, this document seemed to bode well for the presbyterians, since they were generally in favor of the monarch—in contrast to the independents or congregationalists, who were not. Above all, the presbyterians sought complete "comprehension" within the Church of England, in contrast to the independents and congregationalists, who only sought "indulgence" or toleration of their churches, since they wanted to remain separate from the state church. This was one of the major distinctions among the different Puritan groups at this time.

Manton the Negotiator, 1660–62

Within a couple of months of the Declaration of Breda, Parliament resolved to return Charles to the throne. Manton and others traveled to Holland with the invitation. But it was soon apparent that Charles was less interested in establishing the presbyterian cause. In the course of discussions with him, Manton realized this and began to champion (along with his colleague Richard Baxter) modified episco-

CHARLES II.

3.2. Picture of Charles II, whom Manton (and others) invited to return to become King of England in 1660.

pacy, which the episcopalian James Usher had proposed previously in his *The Reduction of the Episcopacy* (1656). Apparently the unity of the church was more important to these divines than the establishment of presbyterianism. Nevertheless, the restoration of Charles II ultimately signaled the defeat of the presbyterian cause. Although the new king did make Manton and several other presbyterians his personal chaplains, Manton, Richard Baxter notes in his autobiography, was never invited to preach before him.

Charles did keep his original promise, however, of entertaining recommendations by the presbyterians. As a result, Baxter and others—Manton included—convened at Sion College in London to draft a document for the new king. Their proposal was moderate. The document outlined three suggestions for reform pertaining to church government, liturgy, and ceremonies. In terms of church government, the document effectively offered little more than a rephrasing of Usher's plan for a modified episcopacy. In fact, the document actually appended Usher's plea by way of his original document. Surprisingly perhaps, historian John Spurr explains, the authors were content to leave Usher's "model of reduced episcopacy 'without a word of alteration.'" When it came to the liturgy, the document called for the removal of the Book of Common Prayer, or at least a more "biblical" revision. And in terms of ceremonies, the document stipulated that all ceremonies not enjoined by Scripture should not be prescribed, and that other ceremonies should be optional.

Their proposals were refused. Instead, as C. G. Bolam explains,

> Attempts were made to buy off the leading Presbyterians with offers of preferment. Baxter was offered the see of Hereford, Calamy that of Lichfield and Coventry, and

Reynolds that of Norwich, while Manton and Bates were offered deaneries.

Only Reynolds accepted the offer. In the spring of the following year (1661), the new king commissioned twelve bishops, convened and led by Gilbert Sheldon, Bishop of London, and twelve presbyterians to meet at the Savoy (Hospital) to review the Book of Common Prayer. There Reynolds, Baxter, Manton, and others discussed with the episcopalians their recommendations for changes to the liturgy. This meeting, however, actually carried far less importance than the proposals the presbyterians had originally drafted at Sion College the year before. This is because the Savoy Conference entertained recommendations only for the revision of the Prayer Book, and not church government. It did not matter, however. The bishops who presided over the meeting saw little need for revision. Moreover, even as the Savoy Conference was in session, the newly elected Parliament—accurately called the Cavalier Parliament as a result of its royalist leanings—attempted to reinstate the Prayer Book of 1604 and sought to pass legislation that opposed the presbyterians.

The beginning of the end of the presbyterian cause was clear. Despite the king's willingness to discuss comprehension of the presbyterians into the state church, the Cavalier Parliament was dominated by Laudians who were inhospitable to the presbyterians and their proposals. The culmination of the new legislation was the Act of Uniformity (1662). This act, as John Spurr describes, "was a blunt instrument by which to define a church." It was "primarily designed to exact conformity" to the Church of England on the basis of four requirements and was directly opposed to the Puritan vision of the church, not least all of the documents that the Westminster Assembly had produced less than two decades before:

- All clergymen were to be (re-)ordained by a bishop.
- They were to disavow the Solemn League and Covenant.
- They were to abide completely by the Prayer Book.
- And they were to subscribe fully to the Thirty-Nine Articles of Religion.

Those who failed to conform to these requirements were to be ejected from their livings on St. Bartholomew's Day, August 24, 1662; this came to be known as the Great Ejection.

Rather than abide by this new law, Manton and countless others resigned. Manton preached his last sermon at Covent Garden on August 17. His sermon was based on Hebrews 12:1, and it contains not a word about the Act of Uniformity or his ejection from the parish. It was a typical exposition of the biblical text, in line with William Perkins's own exegetical methodology, which directly explained the text while indirectly addressing the social issues it encompassed. Manton's sermon, along with many others by nonconformists, was published in 1662. Altogether, more than 2,000 ministers holding office or a living in the Church of England were ejected; approximately 7,000 conformed. Although the king made preparations later that year by means of the Declaration of Indulgence for religious liberty, the presbyterians generally disapproved of the proposal since they perceived that it was animated by Roman Catholic sentiments rather than Protestant ones.

The new legislation passed by Parliament effectively ended the presbyterian cause in England. In fact, as Charles Whiting explains, the very term *presbyterian* was loosely applied in popular language "to all those who went out between 1660 and 1662 rather than accept the episcopal system." With the return to the episcopacy, presbyterianism would find expression in colonial America, and Scotland in particular. Although vestiges of presbyterianism remained in the London area, Manton is rightly regarded as one of the last old presbyterians in all of England.

Manton the Nonconformist, 1662–77

Thomas Manton was a moderate dissenter. He desperately wanted comprehension into the Church of England, and he dedicated the later years of his life toward that end. As a dissenter, he had become what he despised: He was now no different than a Quaker or another sectarian, who he believed undermined the church's unity. Indeed, observes Spurr, "The Presbyterians legitimately felt that they had lost most in 1662." This loss is even more evident given that Manton could have been a prominent figure within English society had he conformed.

Given his prominence, the king offered Manton the deanery of Rochester on the condition of his conformity to the new bill in 1662. This was not an unreasonable offer, and there were many presbyterians who complied with the new changes. Manton did not. Although he refused to conform and declined the king's offer, Manton did continue to worship in the parish of Covent Garden. As Bolam explains,

> The Presbyterians ejected in 1662 found difficulty in reconciling themselves to the idea of being separatists. Many of them still regarded themselves as members of the Church of England and continued to attend parish worship.

Manton was one such person, and he actually attended the services of his successor at Covent Garden, Simon Patrick (who remained there until he became Bishop of Ely in 1689), until he was eventually accused by Patrick of slander and of circulating libel among the congregation. Later, in 1669, Manton was censured by Humphrey Henchman, Bishop of London, for refusing Communion.

Manton spent the rest of his life in a struggle between nonconformity and conformity. Although he continued to pursue comprehension into the Church of England, a spate of legislative acts by the Cavalier Parliament in the 1660s militated against this—including the following: the Corporation Act (1661), Act of Uniformity (1662), First Conventicle Act (1664), and the Five Mile Act (1665). Each of these Acts, which are all part of the Clarendon Code (so named after Edward Hyde, Earl of Clarendon), was designed to oppose religious assemblages outside the Church of England and to prohibit dissenting ministers from preaching.

The acts deliberately attempted to suppress dissenters. As Spurr notes, however, "the 'Clarendon Code' was failing to reduce the Dissenters to uniformity." Instead the opposite was occurring. Many presbyterian ministers and nonconformists risked censure and even imprisonment for the opportunity to preach. Manton's more famous contemporary John Bunyan (1628–88), for instance, was imprisoned several times for violating the Clarendon Code, as was Richard Baxter. Moreover, after his imbroglio with Simon Patrick at Covent Garden, Manton also began preaching, as Harris notes, "on the Lord's-day evenings in his own house to his family, and some few of his neighbours; and sometime after, on Wednesday mornings, when the violence of the times would allow it."

Manton continued to preach illegally even while remaining in the king's favor and attempting comprehension. He is doubtless one of those nonconformist clergy who, as Spurr describes, "clearly kept a foot in both camps." In 1668 Charles II met at Lord Arlington's residence with Manton and others to discuss an agreement between the presbyterians and the established church, as well as limited toleration for independents. The meeting, however, did not result in success, as apparently John Owen wrecked the discussion in his insistence upon complete toleration for the independents. Owen did this because he was mindful that comprehension of the presbyterians into the national church would leave the independents vulnerable. In this way, Manton and Owen agreed to differ with regard to convictions about the unity of the church.

For the next few years presbyterians like Manton continued to preach in their homes and other private venues. Manton also entered into discussion with other nonconformists such as independents and baptists about resistance to the Conventicle Act. It is for these reasons that he was ultimately arrested in 1670 on a Sunday afternoon immediately after delivering his sermon (since anyone who refused to take the Oxford Oath was prohibited from preaching). His imprisonment, however, was brief in comparison to others—it lasted only six months—and he was treated with deference and leniency as a result of his stature and disposition. Upon his release, Manton continued preaching illegally, this time at White Hart Yard. He barely escaped a second arrest due to a timely warning by James Bedford, who had taken the Oxford Oath and was therefore legally able to preach. Religious persecution of this type continued, which in turn created division; as a result, Manton's peacemaking skills were desperately needed to unite the divided presbyterian camp.

There were effectively two camps within presbyterianism at this unstable time. The first camp, called the "dons," was comprised of older presbyterians like Manton and William Bates. These older clergymen sought comprehension in the Church of England. They were also much better connected to the upper classes and nobility, which explains in part why they were harassed less than others who espoused similar theologies. The second camp, labeled the "ducklings," referred to the younger presbyterians who, like the independents, Spurr explains, "did not dream of a role in a national church but saw their future in terms of an autonomous denomination." Rather than comprehension in the established church, in other words, they desired indulgence or toleration. The ducklings were naturally much less connected politically. The division of these two camps was an important one, since those who sought only indulgence were suspicious of the dons who eagerly intended comprehension.

Momentous developments both politically and religiously occurred in 1672. The king was preparing for battle along with France against the Dutch, and the arrangement with Louis XIV of France partially entailed Charles II's conversion to Roman Catholicism. The result was Charles's issuance in the spring of that year of the important *Declaration of Indulgence*, which allowed nonconformists such as the presbyterians and independents the ability to congregate publicly and for their ministers to preach legally upon obtaining a license. Altogether approximately 1,500 English ministers received licenses to preach once more, most of which were presbyterians like Manton. The issuance additionally permitted Roman Catholics to worship legally in their homes.

Although the Roman Catholic intention of the indulgence produced consternation among the presbyterians, they were grateful for the opportunity to worship freely as they had been able to do only a few years previously. Presbyterians like Manton enthusiastically embraced the opportunity to lecture and preach legally, and he was licensed to preach as a presbyterian at his home in Covent Garden in April of that year (1672). Shortly thereafter Manton became one of six lecturers appointed to preach at Pinners' Hall in London. This was, as Peter Toon explains, "a joint

Presbyterian-Congregationalist Lecture," which included the finest and most respected Puritan preachers in all of England: William Bates, William Jenkyn, Thomas Manton, Richard Baxter, John Collins, and John Owen.

The lectureship at Pinners' Hall continued to operate for many years despite the fact that Parliament rescinded the king's *Declaration of Indulgence* only a year after Charles issued it, arguing that it was illegal. Due in part both to the number of important figures this lecture hall attracted and to the respectability of the lecturers involved, interference from authorities appears to have been minimal. Although the Lord Mayor was aware of the gathering, he did not seek to close it, and in fact it only ended as a result of internal disagreements. Manton himself remained a regular preacher there until his death. He also preached on occasion at Cripplegate, a well-known Puritan stronghold in London, in addition to giving many sermons at his home in Covent Garden—mostly to his aristocratic followers, many of whom were women.

One of Manton's last sermons before his death, preached at Cripplegate in the year 1675, was entitled "The Scripture Sufficient without Unwritten Traditions." In the sermon Manton reproved the Roman Catholics since

> they cry up a private, unproved, unwritten tradition of their own, as of equal authority with this safe and full rule which is contained in the written word of God.

Nevertheless, "though we blame this in Papists," he concludes, "yet we reject not all tradition," namely, the tradition of Scripture itself. Manton's very typical Protestant critique against Rome in this sermon coincides with the increasing intolerance of the Roman Catholic religion at this time in England's history. As Michael Watts remarks,

From 1673 onwards many Anglicans became increasingly alarmed at the signs of growing Catholic influence at court, and especially at the prospect of Charles II's being succeeded by his brother, the now openly Roman Catholic James, Duke of York, and as Anglican fears of Catholicism increased, so their hostility to Dissent abated.

WILLIAM III.

3.3. Portrait of William III, who became the King of England with his wife, Mary, in 1689.

It is in this context that Baxter, Manton, Bates, and Matthew Poole (1624–79) once again made concerted efforts at comprehension into the established church in 1675. These men, united with their Anglican counterparts by an equally strong opposition to Roman Catholicism, continued to seek unity with the Church of England.

The negotiations, however, ended poorly for the nonconformists yet again. As Harold Wood explains, "Tentative terms that were drawn up by Baxter ('An Healing Act,' he termed it) were submitted to those bishops, who promptly disapproved them." The end of persecution and the complete toleration of dissenters would not be realized for more than a decade, well after Manton's death in 1677. After the Glorious Revolution of 1688 expelled the despised and pro-Catholic King James II (1633–1701) from power in exchange for the non-Catholic co-reigns of William and Mary (1689–94), wider toleration for the Protestant nonconformist was imminent. Indeed, as Spurr points out, "The Church of England was the greatest loser from the Revolution of 1688," since its unity and authority were undermined.

Conclusion: Manton the Peacekeeper

Thomas Manton died on October 18, 1677, at the age of fifty-seven, a decade before these momentous changes. His health had begun to decline around 1675. He was survived by his wife, Mary Morgan (d. 1701), and three children. Manton's great popularity in the London area is attested by both the quantity as well as the religious diversity of the people who attended his funeral. As Caroline Richardson notes,

> [James] Usher's popularity may be explained in part by his conspicuous position, which brought him into contact with many people; but Dr. Thomas Manton the presbyterian,

who had no extraordinary opportunities to impress the public, also won general approval and liking. When he died (Ralph Thoresby writes in his *Diary*), this preacher, "deservedly styled the King of Preachers," had a funeral "attended with the vastest number of ministers of all persuasions, etc., that ever I saw together in my life. And the Ministers walking in pairs, a Conformist and a Nonconformist."

This description embodies the legacy of Thomas Manton for three reasons. First, Manton is correctly remembered first and foremost as a preacher. Preaching was both his passion and his only profession. Unlike his more scholastic contemporary John Owen, for instance, who bequeathed approximately the same number of completed volumes to posterity as Manton had done, Manton never produced any dogmatic works or taught at the university. On the contrary, his writings are exclusively expositions of Scripture—all practical in nature—which he preached to various audiences from 1640 until his death in 1677. In this way it is completely appropriate that Ralph Thoresby, a nonconformist who moved to London in 1677 and immediately began writing a diary, regarded Manton as the "King of Preachers."

Second, Manton was a presbyterian. At least since his arrival to the London area in 1645, Manton dedicated the entirety of his life to the establishment of presbyterianism in England. He did this, as he explained in one of his sermons preached before Parliament in the 1640s, because he believed that presbyterianism was the surest course to take for reform. His participation in the Westminster Assembly as well as his involvement in the classis movement in London further illustrates this disposition toward presbyterianism. It was also as a presbyterian—and not, for instance, as a congregationalist or baptist like Owen or Bunyan respectively—that Manton relentlessly pursued comprehension into the Church of England. Although this never occurred, he never abandoned what Toon describes as "the fine ideal of the one Church containing all the Protestant Christians and ministers of the nation."

Finally, Thoresby's report above that described both nonconformist and conformist alike at Manton's funeral epitomizes his life as an irenicist. Just like his good friend Richard Baxter, Manton's contemporaries commonly regarded him as conciliatory and irenic. His peacemaking skills had been required many times throughout the course of his life—with Charles II, with episcopalians, with congregationalists, even with sectarians and Jews—and Manton maintained friendships with numerous individuals of divergent points of view. In fact, as the *Oxford Dictionary of National Biography* states,

> Manton was the most popular of the presbyterians, and used his influence "for the public tranquillity." Bates says "his prudent, pacific spirit rendered him most useful in these divided times." . . . He made no enemies.

Manton was regarded by his peers as honorable and pacifying. In the funeral sermon that he preached at Manton's death, William Bates described his deceased colleague in the following terms:

> He was no fomenter of faction, but studious of the public tranquillity. He knew what a blessing peace is, and wisely foresaw the pernicious consequences that attend divisions.

Shortly after his death, Manton's last sayings were published in the winter of 1677. This document, entitled *Words of Peace*, contains Manton's sayings both throughout his lifetime and especially on his deathbed. These sayings or proverbs, a total of fifty in all, summarize Manton's life and reflect his personal views of his own career and religious purity and unity. The last words of an English divine, who lived through one of the most troublesome periods of religious strife in England's history, lifted up peace and reconciliation:

> Provided that people agree in Religious principles, let them never be like the *Bulls of Bashan*, Goring and Wounding each other.
>
> Tis fatal to Religion, when once we cry up *Names*, and those names beget *Parties*, for then men look to accommodate their own faction, though it be to the hazard of religion and publique peace.
>
> To smite with the hand is beneath a man, *to smite with the Tongue* beneath a Christian, and yet how often are Christians guilty of both *biting and devouring one another*.
>
> Some men love to live in the fire, and be always handling the red hot questions of the Age with passion and Acrimony: but alas! this does no good.
>
> There may be diverse colours, but there should be no Rent in the Churches Coat.
>
> Tis good to preserve truth, but small distempers need not violent cures; he's a *mad man* that fires his house to destroy the Mice in it.

As these proverbs indicate, Thomas Manton lived during an extremely difficult and unstable time in England's history, and his dying words were doubtlessly voiced out of lived experience. His life and works, though previously obscured, should be brought to life, so that future Christians may have access to his words of wisdom and words of eloquence.

PART TWO

MANTON AS BIBLICAL INTERPRETER: HIS COMMENTARY ON JAMES

N ow that the social and historical context in which Thomas Manton lived has been thoroughly explored, it is now appropriate to examine his most important writings. As we do so, it will become readily apparent that Manton's writings are exclusively expositions of Scripture, all of which reside in his twenty-two-volume corpus of writings. These expositions, most of which he originally preached at various locations including churches, lecture halls, homes, and Parliament between the years of 1640 and 1677, encompass both the Old and New Testaments. Manton preferred to preach verse-by-verse, usually a specific chapter or select number of chapters at a time. Some of the more noteworthy sermon series that he preached include: the Lord's Prayer (vol. 1), Isaiah 53 (vol. 3), eighteen sermons on 2 Thessalonians 2 (vol. 3), James (vol. 4), Jude (vol. 5), 190 sermons on Psalm 119 (vols. 6–9), twenty-seven sermons on Matthew 25 (vols. 9–10), forty-two sermons on John 17 (vols. 10–11), twenty-four sermons on Romans 6 and forty-seven sermons on Romans 8 (vols. 11–12), forty sermons on 2 Corinthians 5 (vols. 12–13), and sixty-five sermons on Hebrews 11 (vols. 13–15).

There are a variety of ways to explore Manton's writings in order to discern how and why he wrote what he did. The approach taken in this book is to focus on Manton's most well-known writings rather than his obscure ones. As such, this new section, Part Two, concentrates on his sermons or commentary on the Letter of James, while the next section, Part Three, looks at some of his other important sermons throughout his career. The specific way that we will analyze his commentary on James is by setting it in juxtaposition to other biblical expositions that were written immediately before, during, and after Manton's life. By putting Manton's commentary in conversation with his contemporaries', we will better understand the distinctives of his approach.

There are four reasons why this second section concentrates on Manton's commentary on James rather than others. First, in order to become familiar with the manner in which Manton interpreted Scripture, it is arguably better to isolate one complete biblical text rather than several incomplete texts. This allows us to see continuity in Manton's writing, as we see him cover a multitude of issues within the context of one document. James has therefore been selected for this purpose, since it is the only biblical text that Manton fully interpreted and commented on except for Jude, which is a short and historically neglected book.

Second, according to his biographer William Harris, Manton's commentary on James was superior to Jude in both content and method. The commentary on Jude, "though excellent in its kind," writes Harris, "is not so strictly expository, but more in a sermon way, which [Manton] says was more in compliance with the desires of others than with his own judgment." What is more, Manton's commentary on

James happens to be the first commentary that Manton had published (in 1651).

Third, Manton's exposition of James illustrates more abundantly than others his use of the interpretive tradition before him. As Hughes Oliphant Old explains,

> This commentary is clearly the result of careful and disciplined study of the whole history of the interpretation of the book of James.

Manton's commentary on James represents a verse-by-verse exposition of the entire epistle, encompassing roughly 500 pages. This exposition, which Manton began and completed during his weekday lectures at Stoke Newington, Middlesex early in his career during the late 1640s, interacts more extensively with previous and contemporary sources than his other sermonic expositions. In this way it serves as an appropriate text for detailed study of Manton's use of and interaction with other authors.

Finally, the exposition of James has been selected from Manton's greater corpus because of the controversy surrounding this biblical letter throughout the history of the church. This controversy, which emerged first in the early church and most recently after Martin Luther's appropriation of the epistle, was by no means unknown to Manton. In fact, Manton defended the integrity and canonicity of the epistle vigorously against those who argued otherwise, and his commentary made great use of the tradition's interpretation of this text. Manton's commentary on James therefore serves as an appropriate means of study through which to evaluate his interpretative method and his use of the exegetical tradition. It shows Manton at his finest.

In short, this section suggests itself as a fine way to introduce readers to Manton in general and Puritan biblical interpretation in particular. Each of the chapters in this section focuses on different aspects of James. These themes or topics have been selected based on Manton's own inclination toward them, which is evident in his commentary. Although he commented on the entire text of James, he—as well as the interpretive tradition before him—focused considerable attention on the three sections below, which revolved around the themes of authorship and canonicity (James 1), salvation or soteriology (2:14–26), and church government or ecclesiology (5:14–16). Specifically in this section, Chapter 4 concentrates on Manton's interpretation of James 1:1 in relation to Protestant reformers; Chapter 5 focuses on his interpretation of James 2:14–26 in relation to Puritans; and, finally, Chapter 6 concentrates on Manton's interpretation of James 5:14–16 in relation to Anglicans.

4

Manton and the Reformers on James 1:1: Jostling James into the Canon

It was quite typical in both the Reformation and the era of orthodoxy for biblical interpreters to begin their commentaries with sections identified as *argumenta* ["arguments"] or as analyses of the scope or focus and argumentative shape (*methodus*) of the whole book.

Richard Muller

[A]s to the author [of this epistle], there is . . . reason for doubting.

John Calvin

Of late, I confess, [the Letter of James] has found harder measure. Cajetan and Erasmus show little respect to it; Luther plainly rejects it; and for the incivility and rudeness of his expression in calling it *stramineam epistolam* ["an epistle of straw"], as it cannot be denied, so it is not to be excused.

Thomas Manton

Introduction

Although he (intentionally) never wrote a formal commentary on the letter as he did on many others in the New Testament, Martin Luther's (1483–1546) notorious comments about the Epistle of James—chiefly, that it was an "epistle of straw"—became a byword in the interpretive tradition by the mid-sixteenth century. In fact, nearly every interpreter who commented on the letter after the time of Luther, whether Catholic or Protestant, did so in full awareness of Luther's comments and responded accordingly—and almost always negatively. When Thomas Manton wrote his commentary on James in the 1640s, for example, he reserved his most bitter remarks for Luther. He regarded the reformer's comments, a century past, as "rude," "uncivil," and even "blasphemous."

Dissatisfaction with and disapproval of Luther's appraisal of James was widespread and immediate, and the subsequent recovery of the letter's significance within the canon occurred over the course of several decades, of which Manton's commentary served as the culmination of this lengthy process. Protestant interpreters during and immediately after the Reformation illustrate this process well as they variously commented on James subsequent to Martin Luther. After first discussing Luther's own interpretation of James, this chapter focuses on how individual commentators among the three most dominant Protestant traditions at this time—Reformed, Lutheran, and Anglican—responded to Luther's comments. Specifically, this chapter explains how John Calvin (1509–64), Niels Hemmingsen (1513–1600), and Thomas Manton (1620–77) collectively and completely distanced themselves from Luther's (perceived) negative comments about the Letter of James. In fact, Manton serves as the culmination of this criticism against Luther, and it plainly illustrates how the Englishmen interpreted the Letter of James. By focusing on Manton's reaction to Luther (in conversation with interpreters after the German reformer), this chapter, in short, serves as the first of three that discuss Manton's most well-known and well-respected work, his commentary on James, by explaining his method of interpreting this book in relation to his contemporaries.

4.1. Portrait of Martin Luther by his friend Lucas Cranach.

Martin Luther (1483–1546)

Martin Luther first publicly questioned the integrity of the Letter of James within the context of his famous discussion of the sacraments in *The Babylonian Captivity of the Church* in the fall of 1520. This was one of several important writings that the reformer wrote in that year. Specifically, in reference to the so-called sacrament of extreme unction, which Catholic priests administered to those who were sick or dying, Luther attacked the doctrine's biblical basis by suggesting—as did the Catholic priests and the scholars Erasmus (1466–1536) just before him and Cajetan (1469–1534) soon afterward—that "this epistle is not by James the apostle, and that it is not worthy of an apostolic spirit." However, in his argument against extreme unction, Luther left the question of authorship aside and argued instead that extreme unction was not a sacrament on other grounds—namely, because it lacked dominical institution, that is, a direct command from the Lord in the Gospels.

It was not until two years later, in 1522, that Luther published his most famous comments on James. These remarks, which emerged in the context of Luther's translation of the New Testament into German, have been notoriously intertwined with the reformer ever since. In the conclusion to his prefaces to the New Testament, where he commented on various books and explained his method of biblical interpretation, Luther offered these final remarks:

> In a word, St. John's Gospel and his first epistle, St. Paul's epistles, especially Romans, Galatians, and Ephesians, and St. Peter's first epistle are the books that show you Christ and teach you all that is necessary and salvific for you to know, even if you were never to see or hear any other book of doctrine. Therefore, St. James' epistle is really an epistle of straw [*stramineam epistolam*; German: *ein rechte stroern*

Epistel], compared to these others, for it has nothing of the nature of the gospel about it.

Although Luther later removed these comments from the 1534 preface in the complete Bible and, in 1539, from printings of the New Testament (most importantly, his comment about James being "an epistle of straw"), they generated widespread discussion and opprobrium among subsequent interpreters, and they have since then become a byword in the exegetical tradition.

Luther's comments on James, up to this point, largely (but not completely) reflected the views of his Catholic contemporaries Erasmus and Cajetan. Luther, however, differed considerably from these two theologians in at least one important way. Whereas Erasmus and Cajetan questioned the authorship of James based on linguistic and historical grounds (from a tradition stretching all the way back to church fathers Eusebius and Jerome), Luther, in addition to these two reasons, questioned the letter's apostolicity (the book's status as coming from an apostle) and canonicity (its authorized status as a book in the Bible) on the basis of its theology. As New Testament scholar Luke Timothy Johnson explains in his commentary on James,

> Luther pushed the principle of *[S]achkritik* ("content criticism") to the extreme of rejecting James entirely because of its (perceived) contradiction to Luther's fundamental principle of *sola fide* [faith alone].

Indeed, as Luther himself states in his preface to the Epistles of James and Jude in 1522, "I do not regard [James] as the writing of an apostle."

Luther offered three main reasons why he questioned James. First, he argues, the epistle "is flatly against St. Paul and all the rest of Scripture in ascribing justification to works." When understood within Luther's well-known respect for and privileging of Paul's letters in general and his doctrine of justification by faith in particular, he construed the Letter of James as directly opposing both Paul and Scripture. Second, he continues, although "[the book's] purpose is to teach Christians . . . in all [its] long teaching it does not mention the Passion, the resurrection, or the Spirit of Christ." Finally, the reformer concludes, "James does nothing more than drive to the law and to its works." For these reasons, Luther summarizes,

> I cannot include him among the chief books, though I would not thereby prevent anyone from including or extolling him as he pleases, for there are otherwise many good sayings in him.

Although Luther referred to James on numerous occasions throughout the remainder of his career, these comments from *The Babylonian Captivity to the Church* in 1520 and, especially, the prefaces to the New Testament and the Letter of James in 1522 encapsulate well Luther's (complex) view of James. As David Lotz explains in an article on Luther's method of biblical interpretation: Because Luther "uses the principle 'what preaches Christ' to determine the boundaries of the biblical canon," he concludes that James is not apostolic. However, contrary to popular thinking, Luther does not reject James completely or even partially. On the contrary, he considers it a fine letter and includes it in the canon; but he sees it as inferior to the "the right and precious books" of the New Testament, namely, Paul's letters and the Gospels. Indeed, the very fact that Luther calls James an epistle "of straw," which language he adopts from Paul in 1 Corinthians 3:10–15, indicates that he does not reject it. Just as Paul's metaphor about a building that is constructed by gold or silver is better than one constructed by hay or straw, so books of the New Testament like Romans and John (gold) are superior to books like James or Jude (straw)—but these lesser ones are certainly not worthless.

Despite his intentions, however, and his otherwise favorable or at least neutral statements about the letter, those who interpreted James after Luther gravitated toward those comments he made that questioned the integrity of James. It is for this reason, perhaps, why so few Lutheran exegetes wrote commentaries on the letter. Aside from Luther's former German theological ally Andreas von Karlstadt (1486–1541), who disagreed with Luther about the status and importance of James and who even attacked his view, German Lutherans after Luther did not generally write commentaries on the letter. Luther made it very clear, in other words, that other books in the New Testament provided better theology.

John Calvin (1509–64)

In the Protestant exegetical tradition, the writing of commentaries on James fell to the Reformed. Chief among the Reformed commentators was John Calvin, who wrote commentaries on all of the New Testament, excluding Revelation and 2 and 3 John. Calvin published his Latin commentary on the Catholic Epistles in 1551, and although he dedicated it to Edward VI and it appears to have been well received in England, it was not translated into English during the sixteenth century. Although Calvin had less of an aversion than Luther did to books like Hebrews, James, and Jude, Calvin did position 1 Peter and 1 John before James among the Catholic Epistles, and he did not even deign to include 2 and 3 John in his commentaries. Calvin's decision to give canonical prominence to 1 Peter and 1 John in terms of positioning was not atypical; the Latin Vulgate, originating in the fourth century under Jerome, had done this. However, his decision not to write on 2 and 3 John doubtlessly reflects the elasticity of the canon in the first half of the sixteenth century.

As Richard Muller explains in relation to Luther in the second of his four-volume work on Reformed theology, so too is the case for Calvin and his contemporaries:

> Luther's famous and highly hyperbolic dismissal of the Epistle of James as an epistle of "straw" can easily be set into an early Reformation context in which the patristic distinction between *homologoumena* [recognized books] and *antilegomena* [disputed ones] in the New Testament still functioned. This sense of the relative fluidity of canon rapidly gave way in the sixteenth century to a stricter sense of

4.2. Portrait of John Calvin, the famous Protestant theologian of Geneva.

the equally normative value of all the books of the New Testament, indeed, of the Bible as a whole.

Harry Gamble confirms this: "[N]o ecumenical authority of the ancient church ever rendered a formal decision for the church at large as to the exact contents of the Christian scripture." It would not be until later in the sixteenth century when statements of faith like the Belgic and Helvetic Confessions officially closed the canon in the Reformed Protestant tradition.

Even though Calvin worked during a time in which the canon was more fluid, the "stricter sense" of the "equally normative value of all the books of the New Testament" emerges in the thought of Calvin in a way that it does not in Luther. In his argument for the Epistle of James, for instance, Calvin writes:

> It appears from the writings of Jerome and Eusebius, that this Epistle was not formerly received by many Churches without opposition. There are also at this day some [namely, Luther] who do not think it entitled to authority. I am happy, however, to receive it without controversy, because I see no just cause for rejecting it.

Whereas Luther rejected the apostolicity of the Letter of James as a result of its reticence about the passion of Christ—indeed, hardly any mention of Jesus at all—and its fondness for law rather than gospel, Calvin accepted the letter. Interestingly, the reasons Calvin gives for accepting the letter—namely, that James and Paul are reconcilable, and that James's reserve in speaking about Christ is consonant with Scripture—appeal not to the church's authority but to Calvin's personal hermeneutic. It also reveals how closely he had read Luther's arguments and, by rejecting them, honored them as worthy of reply.

For Calvin, the deciding factor for determining the authority of James was not that it must preach Christ. Certainly Calvin believed that Scripture did this, but he understood the canon differently. The criterion is "that it contains nothing unworthy of an Apostle of Christ." In other words, whereas Luther viewed the canon more positively (Scripture must preach Christ), Calvin regarded it more negatively (Scripture must not oppose Christ's teachings). Moreover, in contrast to Luther (who additionally disfavored James for its stress on law and practical instruction), Calvin favors it. In the words of the Genevan reformer, "It is indeed full of instruction on various subjects, the benefit of which extends to every part of the Christian life." For Calvin, in other words, the problem with James is not internal; it is a perfectly useful and "Christian" book. The problem is more external: Who is the author of this epistle?

This last component to Calvin's argument raises the important historical question of authorship. Calvin writes, "As to the author, there is . . . more reason for doubting [the authority of the letter]." Historically, the exegetical tradition had concluded that there were three potential Jameses: James of Zebedee and James of Alpheus, who were among the twelve apostles, and James the Just, the brother of the Lord. As Calvin confirms,

> The ancients are nearly unanimous in thinking that [the author of James] was one of the disciples named [Just] and a relative [note: not brother] of Christ, who was set over the Church at Jerusalem.

This was the James, Calvin further explains, whom the ancients believed Paul referred to in Galatians.

Calvin disagreed with the tradition, however. As he explains: "[the notion] that one of the disciples was mentioned as one of the three pillars, and thus exalted above the other Apostles, does not seem to me probable." Calvin suggests that Paul refers to "the son of Alpheus" rather than James the Just, the Bishop of Jerusalem. This is because Calvin does not understand how a nonapostle (that is, one of the Twelve) such as James the Just could be cited in Scripture as somehow superior to the other two Jameses, who were apostles. For this reason, Calvin concludes his argument indecisively: "[which] of the two [James of Alpheus or James the Just] was the writer of this Epistle, it is not for me to say." In the end, however, the identity of the author matters little to Calvin. What is important is the content of the letter, which he interprets as full of "remarkable passages" on various significant issues in "the Christian life." In other words, James is canonical, and justly so, because it does not oppose Christ's teachings.

Niels Hemmingsen (1513–1600)

Although he was not the first Reformed theologian to write a formal commentary on James, John Calvin's work was incorporated into the Protestant exegetical tradition in the sixteenth century in a way that other Reformed commentaries were not. This is not exactly the case with Niels Hemmingsen. Hemmingsen, a bishop, scholar, and influential Lutheran preacher in his native Denmark, is certainly not as recognized today as his Protestant contemporary John Calvin, but he was an important figure. Indeed, as Kenneth Hagen explains in a chapter on biblical interpretation in the sixteenth century:

Hemmingsen (1513–1600) was not unknown in sixteenth-century Europe. He was at the center of university and church life in Denmark. The *praeceptor universalis Daniae* was also the leader in the Philipist period of power. The "brilliant young Dane" was with Melanchthon in Wittenberg,

1537–42; then in Copenhagen (1542) as professor of Greek (1543), dialectic (1545), and theology (1553), until his dismissal in 1579 on grounds of Crypto-Calvinism regarding the Lord's Supper. Tyrgve Skarsten says that "his fame and reputation throughout the learned circles of Europe brought renown and glory to the University of Copenhagen. His Latin and Danish works were to be found in the leading libraries in multiple editions and often in Dutch, English, and German translation."

It is surely noteworthy that Hemmingsen's commentary on James was translated into English and Calvin's was not. It appeared in English in 1577, with the Latin original preceding it by five years. Hemmingsen's commentary begins with an "argument" or explanation of the letter, which had been standard practice since the patristic period. In it the Dane alludes to the controversy surrounding the issue of authorship and apostolicity within the exegetical tradition. Throughout his commentary he assumes, as did the majority of the tradition, that James the Just, Jesus' brother, was the author: "The author of this Epistle was James the Apostle, who is called the brother of the Lord." As Calvin summarized in his argument on James, the collective tradition agreed that James the Just was the author, who may also have been James of Alpheus, but who was clearly not James of Zebedee (whom Herod killed in the early 40s). In contrast to Calvin, however, Hemmingsen agreed with the tradition; and just as the tradition used the standard view of authorship to affirm the authority of the letter against those who questioned it, so Hemmingsen argued forcefully for its apostolicity and authority.

Hemmingsen proceeds to defend the apostleship of James the author by explaining that on the day of Pentecost he was "again by a visible sign authorized and confirmed in his apostleship." More pointedly, he argues: "Here it appears what is to be judged of this Epistle, namely, that we must give no less credit to it than to the voice of God." The two decades that separated Calvin's commentary from Hemmingsen's were significant ones, as the previous "fluidity of the canon" had solidified even more in Protestant doctrine. Whereas Calvin remained somewhat intransigent to the view that James was not apostolic, Hemmingsen was noticeably opposed to this. This explains his defensive posture toward the view that this letter does not comes from "the voice of God." Hemmingsen made this statement to affirm the letter's authority against those who were giving "less credit to it." It is not possible to identify unmistakably to whom Hemmingsen was reacting, but Luther is the most likely candidate. Having studied in Wittenberg the same time Luther taught there, and being so connected with Luther's faithful colleague and supporter Philip Melanchthon (1497–1560), Hemmingsen was surely familiar with Luther's view of James.

Hemmingsen concludes his argument with a traditional discussion on the meaning of the term "Catholic Epistles." Of significance in this closing section is his discussion of the canon. In the context of distinguishing the letters of Paul from the other New Testament writings, Hemmingsen writes that "whatsoever we read in the Epistles of the Apostles, we ought to embrace it as a canon or rule of the truth." In other words, he concludes, the Epistle of James (as well as the rest of the Catholic Epistles) remains canonical and authoritative—regardless of doubts in regard to authorship and historical circumstance.

Thomas Manton (1620–77)

In contrast to several commentaries that Reformed theologians on the European Continent wrote on James, and less occasional ones that Lutherans composed, very few English divines published commentaries on James during the sixteenth century. By the time of the mid-seventeenth century, however, several interpreters had written commentaries on the letter, the most detailed of which was written by Thomas Manton while he was pastoring the congregation at Stoke Newington, outside of London.

As Manton began writing and lecturing on James in the mid-1640s, the comments that various writers made within the exegetical tradition were more than relevant. In his introduction to James, in fact, he engages each of the most influential commentators on the letter throughout the tradition: Eusebius, Jerome, Bede, Erasmus, Cajetan, Calvin, Hugo Grotius, and especially Luther. In terms of method, Manton stands in the tradition of Hemmingsen regarding style and posture. Overall, in fact, Manton's commentary could be characterized as defensive. He responds decisively to the tradition, stretching back from the time of Eusebius and Jerome to, most recently and, in his view, most scandalously, the time of Luther. In fact, Luther's comments about the Letter of James—a century past—are as provocative as the decade he wrote them. Manton goes to great lengths to prove that James is authoritative, that an apostle did write it, and that it is eminently relevant to the times in which he lives.

Manton's defensive posture characterizes in part the way he handles his introduction and James 1:1. Manton organizes his introductory discussion about the letter around six questions:

1. Whether this epistle is of divine authority?
2. Concerning the subordinate author or instrument, James, what James was this?
3. What was the time of writing it?
4. The persons to whom it was written?
5. What is the occasion, matter, and scope of it?
6. The reason of that term in the title, *catholic* or *general.*

The first question, arguably most important, indicates Manton's defensive posture—questioning whether the letter is of "divine authority." The remaining questions, of less importance than the first, need not be discussed here, since the first question adequately sets the tone for much of Manton's aggressive exposition as well as his close engagement with the overall tradition on James—particularly with Luther.

"Concerning the divine authority of this epistle," Manton begins in relation to the first question, "I desire to discuss it with reverence and trembling." He explains that he would have rather omitted this question but since "to conceal known adversaries is an argument of fear and distrust," it is a question of extreme importance. He answers this question by first including the standard or traditional comments and then by reproving those (principally Eusebius and Jerome) who had endeavored "to jostle James out of the canon." Although Eusebius and Jerome made these comments specifically about James (and the other Catholic Epistles), Manton reasons generally that they infringe upon the authority of the rest of Scripture. Unlike Calvin, however, who responds to these doubts about James by examining the letter internally (which Manton eventually does), Manton first appeals to the church councils in the patristic and early medieval periods for proof that James is rightly considered canonical. This is important to note, as it explains how Manton is able to disagree so strongly with Luther and other influential figures: His authority resides in the collective tradition rather than in individual figures like Luther or Calvin.

Aside from Eusebius and Jerome, the remainder of Manton's resolution to the issue of authority focuses on Luther:

> Of late, I confess, [James] has found harder measure. Cajetan and Erasmus show little respect to it; Luther plainly rejects it; and for the incivility and rudeness of his expression in

calling it [*an epistle of straw*], as it cannot be denied, so it is not to be excused.

Manton then cites Luther's Latin preface to James (originally published in German in 1522), which ultimately denies the apostolicity of the letter. To this quotation Manton then adds:

> . . . which was the error and failing of this holy and eminent servant of God; and therein he is followed by others of his own profession: [Andreas] Osiander [1498–1552], [Joachim] Camerarius [1500–1574], [Johannes] Bugenhagen [1485–1558], &c.

Fortunately, Manton concludes, the "blasphemies" of Luther are not perpetuated by the "modern Lutherans, who allow this epistle in the canon."

Manton certainly answers the question of the epistle's divine authority affirmatively. He explains that he will deal with those "reasons which moved Luther to reject this epistle . . . in their proper places," that is, James 2:14–26. Meanwhile, Manton offers the standard responses to the reasons given for questioning the authority of the epistle as found in Calvin and Hemmingsen. Manton specifically follows the defensive posture of Hemmingsen and those after him, though in a more heightened fashion, when it comes to claiming the inspiration of the Scriptures, which closely resembles the statements written in the contemporary Westminster Confession of Faith (1646), which Puritan divines from the Westminster Assembly had written. As the fourth article of the confession states:

> The authority of the holy Scripture, for which it ought to be believed and obeyed, depend[s] not upon the testimony of any man or church, but wholly upon God (who is truth

itself), the Author thereof; and therefore it is to be received, because it is the Word of God.

By the time Manton wrote his commentary at this time, the fluidity of the canon had solidified to such an extent that those who recognized the disputed history of letters like James—even those as authoritative as Martin Luther—were questioning not just the status of the biblical canon but also God, who inspired the writers of the canon in the first place. As the statement above elucidates, all of Scripture—the Letter of James included, of course—depends solely upon God's authorship of it, regardless of the human instrument God used in the process.

Conclusion

Beginning with John Calvin, it is clear that the Genevan reformer was less interested and less confident about determining the question of authorship. And he was equally less concerned about the question of authority, though he clearly—if not altogether quietly—disagreed with Luther. For Calvin, James of Alphaeus is most likely the author; but it does not ultimately matter. For Niels Hemmingsen and Thomas Manton, by way of contrast, the issue of authorship was extremely important. They were apologetic. James must be an apostle or the authority or canonicity of the letter is jeopardized. The fluidity of the canon became more and more stabilized with the passing of each year. This is apparent in the Tridentine (Roman Catholic) Council and the early Reformed confessions, namely, the Belgic and Helvetic Confessions, as well as in the Westminster Confession of Faith a century later.

In this respect, the two decades that elapsed between the publication of Calvin's commentary in 1551 and Hemmingsen's in 1572 were extremely significant ones. As the fluidity of the New Testament canon solidified, those books that Luther had relegated to a secondary status—in this case, the Epistle of James—became equal participants of the biblical canon. By the time Manton published his commentary on James exactly 100 years after Calvin, he had settled the question of authorship definitively. Not only was James (of Alphaeus) one of the twelve apostles, but he was also Bishop of Jerusalem (thus James the Just) and cousin to Christ. His letter is therefore apostolic—a clear refutation of the views that Manton perceived Luther to hold.

Thomas Manton's perceived attempt of previous theologians to "jostle James out of the canon" provides a helpful way to understand how he interpreted the Letter of James. First, although Manton as a Puritan was deeply indebted to the key doctrines of the Protestant Reformation, he was not beholden to individual Protestant reformers, or even necessarily to isolated doctrines. Instead he was beholden to the Scriptures. Any attempt, therefore, whether intentional or not, to question the contents of the Bible was completely misguided and, in the case of Luther, "blasphemous."

Second, Manton's desire to preserve good doctrine was not just an academic exercise. Although maintaining good doctrine was essential for Puritans, Manton's interests were more pragmatic. As the title of his commentary indicated, his aim was "practical" in nature. It was intended to relay the Letter of James, understood within the context of the Westminster Confession of Faith to be the very voice of God, to an audience that desperately needed to hear it. It is true that Manton interacted heavily with the tradition before him, but he did so to exhort his hearers. For a Reformed pastor such as himself, this was the most effective way for him to preach the Scriptures and positively encourage his English congregation.

5

MANTON AND THE PURITANS
ON JAMES 2:14–26:
SAVING THE STRAWY EPISTLE

Many sweat hard at reconciling James with Paul . . . but
unsuccessfully. "Faith justifies" [Romans 3:28] stands in flat
contradiction to "Faith does not justify" [James 2:24]. If
anyone can harmonize these sayings, I will put my doctor's
cap on him and let him call me a fool.
Martin Luther

Cryptic or *hidden* passages are those which are difficult and
obscure. For expounding them this rule and guide should be
followed: If the natural meaning of the words obviously
disagrees with either the analogy of faith or very clear parts of
Scripture, then another meaning . . . must be the right one.
William Perkins

Introduction

Throughout the history of the church, commentators on
the Epistle of James have variously reconciled the author's
view on the doctrine of justification with the apostle Paul's

THE COMPLETE WORKS

OF

THOMAS MANTON, D.D.

VOLUME IV.

CONTAINING

A PRACTICAL COMMENTARY, OR AN EXPOSITION, WITH
NOTES, ON THE EPISTLE OF JAMES.

LONDON:
JAMES NISBET & CO., 21 BERNERS STREET.
1871.

5.1. Title page of Manton's Commentary.

by explaining that they were either referring to two different circumstances or that one's works perfected or illustrated one's true faith. Certain interpreters in the sixteenth century, however, opposed the reconciliation of James and Paul. Martin Luther's largely negative remarks on James, for example, were both widespread and enduring. Although post-Reformation Protestants adopted many of Luther's views—most notably, the doctrine of justification by faith alone, which asserts that people are justified before God by faith and not by any works that they perform—they did not reject the authority of James as Luther had done.

This is especially the case for Puritan interpreters like Thomas Manton. Those in the Puritan tradition collectively regarded the letter of James as apostolic (coming directly from an apostle, usually thought to be James, the bishop of Jerusalem and brother of Jesus), canonical (meriting complete acceptance within the New Testament canon), and even theologically significant (offering a thorough critique of empty faith). This chapter illustrates how Puritan commentators like Thomas Manton interpreted a key biblical passage. Although they maintained the centrality of the theological doctrine of justification by faith alone (*sola fide*), they nevertheless defended the canonicity of James based on their equally central hermeneutical doctrine of the analogy of faith (*analogia fidei*), which asserts that Scripture must conform to orthodox teaching. This is especially the case for Thomas Manton, whose commentary on James serves as the focus of this section. As a Puritan interpreter, Manton's use of the analogy of faith determined how he read and applied the Bible.

In this way, even though the controversial section of James 2:14–26—most notably James's words that people are "justified by works and not by faith alone" (James 2:24)—loomed large in the minds of the Puritans, they fully supported the letter due to their prior reasoning (based on the analogy of faith) that (i) God cannot be self-contradictory; (ii) Scripture comes from God; and (iii) therefore Scripture cannot contain contradictions. Puritan commentators in the seventeenth century exemplify this use of the analogy of faith in their commentaries on James. John Mayer (1583–1664), Edward Leigh (1602–71), and Thomas Manton, three of the earliest Puritans who commented on this letter, all reconcile Paul with James in their exegesis of James 2:14–26.

John Mayer (1583–1664)

Though largely forgotten by posterity, John Mayer was one of a few English divines who wrote substantially on the Letter of James during the seventeenth century. Mayer matriculated to Emmanuel College, Cambridge, and there received all of his degrees: BA (1602), MA (1605), BD (1612), and DD (1627). Although a scholar in his own right, Mayer made his work more accessible to laypeople than many of his contemporaries. As the *Oxford Dictionary of National Biography* (*ODNB*) explains, he

> wrote for those who "not being professed Divines, yet, are studious of the Scriptures" . . . Mayer flouted the convention of publishing works of this nature in Latin to restrict their audience to those with the education considered a prerequisite to comprehend such matters. He declared it desirable that the people become as well versed in the fathers and learned doctors of the church as the clergy.

Mayer's two principal works on James are *Interpretation of the Church* (1627) and *Theological Work* (1629), which are identical except that the latter contains a doctrinal section. Although he makes extensive use of the exegetical tradition in his works, Mayer does not simply follow those who had interpreted Scripture before him: "For I hold it vain for any person . . . to square all his expositions according to that which some other has done before him." "It is a true saying," Mayer continues, "No man, how intelligent whatsoever, but may be weak sighted in some things." The best way to interpret Scripture, in Mayer's estimation, is to "choose that exposition chiefly which shall certainly appear to be his meaning that wrote it"; but when the plain sense of Scripture is not apparent, all things are to be interpreted in "respect to the analogy of faith." Mayer's method of biblical interpretation here exemplifies how he approaches the important section on justification. Although he interacts at length with the exegetical tradition, his greater authority is the *analogia fidei*: James's words must be placed within the context of Paul's words and the rest of Scripture.

The Puritan use of the analogy of faith during the era of Protestant orthodoxy is critical to note. As Henry Knapp explains:

> It would be difficult to overestimate the importance of the *analogy of faith* in the post-Reformation orthodox's herme-neutical strategy. Their exegetes consciously followed it, and they expressed and defended it in their theological writings. Yet, in practice, evidence of its use in the exegetical enter-prise is only found in subtle ways.

Mayer is unusual in that he explicitly refers to the analogy of faith in his exegesis of James here, for virtually none of the other commentators do so. This does not imply, however, that these other exegetes do not make use of the analogy of faith; they clearly do so. It completely guides their interpretation of James 2:14–26. To quote Knapp again:

> The analogy of faith dictated that no true interpretation of a text of Scripture could be contrary to the overall

expression of the faith; the true meaning of a passage could not be set in opposition to other general doctrinal aspects of Christian belief.

In the example at hand, this means that James's doctrine of justification by works cannot be the "true meaning" of the passage, since the doctrine of justification by faith alone is, as Luther stated a century before, one of the chief articles of the faith. Thus the meaning of James's words that seemingly contradict the doctrine of justification by faith alone must be interpreted in relation to the *analogia fidei* or, more properly, the *analogia scripturae* ("analogy of Scripture"), which teaches more pointedly that Scripture cannot contradict itself. As William Perkins explains:

> Apparent contradictions in Scripture can often be resolved by realising that the passages deal with different things although the vocabulary may be the same, or they may be dealing with different aspects, or perspectives or even different time frames.

In addition to Mayer's important use of the *analogia fidei*, he also employs the *locus* ("theme" or "topic") method in his biblical exegesis. This method allows him to comment on the important *loci* or themes emerging from James or, in the case of the work under consideration, the difficult ones. His comments on the section at hand (James 2:14–26) are thus dealt with together and not verse by verse. Mayer begins this section as follows:

> From hence [verse 14] to the end of the chapter, there is only one point handled against those, that bearing themselves upon their faith, neglected the works of mercy, to persuade unto which, James has here undertaken.

This whole section, Mayer explains, revolves around one question: What does James mean when he "denies that a man is justified by faith only, and affirms justification by works"?

In his exegesis of this passage, Mayer interacts predominantly with past biblical interpreters Oecumenius (eleventh century) and David Paraeus (1548–1622). He begins by reviewing Oecumenius's interpretation of this passage, who reconciled Paul and James by positing that the words "faith" and "works" both have two meanings. The first meaning of the term "faith," Mayer explains, refers to "a simple consent unto the thing preached that it is true." This is the type of faith James has in mind in this section. It does not lead to salvation. The second meaning of the term "faith" refers to "a consent joined with the affirmation thereof out of an affection, and with obedience." This is the type of faith Paul intends when he writes that a person is justified by faith and not by works (Romans 3:28). This faith leads to salvation.

The reconciliation of Paul and James, however, requires more than distinguishing between the two types of faith. It also requires double meanings in both the words "faith" and "works." As a result, Mayer joins Oecumenius in differentiating between works performed "before baptism" and works performed thereafter. As Mayer explains,

> He who dies immediately after baptism, dies justified by his faith without works, because he had no time to do any; but he who lives and has time to do, is not justified without good works.

The point Mayer is making is not unique to the history of Protestant exegesis: People are justified by faith; works have nothing to do with justification. Nevertheless, those who are truly justified perform good works. The works that follow are the "fruits and effects" of a "saving and justifying faith."

When it comes to understanding how Abraham was justified, both of these meanings are evident. Abraham's faith in the promises of God *resulted* in his justification, whereas the offering of his son Isaac *illustrated* his faith. Mayer, echoing Paraeus, explains that this is an example of synecdoche or metonymy: The term "faith" necessarily includes a working faith, while the term "works" includes works performed in faith. Or, as Mayer's contemporary and the Oxford Professor William Pemble (1591–1623) articulates in his exegesis of this passage:

> . . . concerning the interpretation of the word 'works' used by James when he says that we are justified by works, this we interpret by a metonymy of the effect for the cause: We are justified by a working faith, by that faith which is apt to declare and show itself in all good works.

Mayer's resolution to the discrepancy between faith and works and Paul and James is thus standard Puritan exegetical practice. He explains:

> And this is in a manner all one with the common solution; faith without works truly justifies before God, that is, makes a sinner just by the imputed righteousness of Christ Jesus: but works make a person's faith evident and conspicuous to the world; it being hereby proved, that a person is a true believer, and so accepted as just and righteous before God.

The last major component to Mayer's exegesis of this section is also derivative. This occurs in the context of his discussion about lively and dead faith. Mayer aligns himself with Augustine (354–430) and Oecumenius who distinguish between lively faith, which contains love, and dead faith, which does not. The latter type of faith characterizes the reference to the devils in 2:19. As Mayer explains, mere belief in the "article[s] of our faith . . . does not make one a true believer." Those with a true and "lively" faith love others as proof of their justification. In this way, Mayer concludes, Protestants are "unjustly taxed by the Papists, as crying down good works." On the contrary,

> we press onto good works as much as they, but that we do it upon a true ground, holding, that it is no lively faith that lacks works; they upon a false, holding, that works, together with faith, does justify.

Overall Mayer's interpretation of James 2:14–26 parallels Augustine's and Oecumenius's exegesis of this section. For Augustine, love characterizes true faith, which is accompanied by love and works. Those who have faith without love have no true faith at all. They are like the demons James mentions. True faith works through love for the good of one's neighbor. For Oecumenius, the focus of his exegesis becomes the reconciliation of Paul and James. Though they use the same terms, they refer to different circumstances: Paul to faith before baptism and James to faith after baptism. In the case of Abraham, therefore, each is correct. Paul rightly states that Abraham was justified by faith alone, while James rightly stresses the importance of works since the two are united subsequent to baptism.

Edward Leigh (1602–71)

Unlike Mayer, who is more properly regarded as a pastor-theologian, Edward Leigh was an MP who served as colonel in the English Civil War during the 1640s. He was a gentleman trained in law and well-connected politically. As the *Oxford Dictionary of National Biography* explains, Leigh's "upbringing was notable for its fervent puritanism, which owed much to his stepmother, Ruth Scudamore, and to his university tutor, William Pemble." Pemble was Leigh's tutor at Magdalen Hall, Oxford, where Leigh graduated BA (1620) and MA (1623). Although Leigh wrote a well-known theological work entitled *A Treatise of Divinity* (1646), he went on to comment on the entire New Testament in 1650, from which his annotations on James serve as the basis for this chapter. In line with the genre of annotations on Scripture, Leigh's comments are briefer than Mayer's. Like John Calvin, who consigned his theological remarks to his *Institutes* and his biblical ones to his commentaries, Leigh addresses the biblical text directly while he devotes more attention to theological *loci* or themes in his dogmatic work. Leigh does, however, include comments from previous commentators on James.

Leigh begins his annotations on James 2:14–26 by stating that James speaks "not of a true justifying faith, but of a faith professed only." This standard Puritan explanation of the passage comes from Calvin's commentary. Leigh explains that the grammatical construction of James's statement implies "a most emphatic negation." From there Leigh moves over the next several verses to comment on verse 19. He conjectures that the devils acknowledge four articles of faith: (i) God; (ii) Christ; (iii) the Day of Judgment; and (iv) eternal punishment.

Leigh's reference to the articles of faith sets boundaries for his exegesis of this passage, which will inevitably try to reconcile Paul and James. Although it is possible that Leigh does not intend to imply this in his reference to the articles here, it nevertheless draws attention once more to the important presupposition that Puritan commentators like Leigh held: James is to be interpreted in light of Paul—and not the other way around. The doctrine of justification by faith must be preserved despite James's words to the contrary. As Leigh states in his *A Treatise of Divinity* in the context of his discussion on the twenty-one New Testament epistles:

> [Romans] is first, not in time of writing, but in dignity, because of the majesty of the things it handles, justification and predestination. It is rightly called *Clavis Theologie* ["Key of Theology"], or the epitome of Christian religion.

Due to the Puritan consensus that the scope of Romans is justification by faith and not by works, the difficult (Perkins would call them "cryptic") verses in James 2:14–26, which appear to the contrary, are not interpreted according to their "natural meaning." Moreover, because the presupposition by the Puritans at this time was that Scripture is infallible, this necessitates that the scope of James must not be justification; it must be something else. In this way, the entire discussion is structured under the mind-set that James refers to a false (profession of) faith; thus, there is nothing contrary to Paul. To interpret Paul through the lens of James, by contrast, was to fall outside the bounds of Puritan or orthodox theology. This was the other position within the Church of England during the seventeenth century, which each of the exegetes examined in this chapter rejected. For instance, George Bull (1634–1710), Bishop of St. David's, held this view: "It is more agreeable to reason to explain St Paul by St James than the contrary." Here Bull appeals to reason whereas the Puritans appeal to the analogy of faith, which they believe interprets reason.

This Puritan mind-set determines Leigh's exegesis of James's words about Abraham in 2:21, the next verse he annotates. Leigh adopts the traditional Protestant reading of this passage like Mayer before him by stating that James refers to justification *in foro humano* ("before humanity") rather than *in foro divino* ("before God"): "It is not meant of the justification of his person before God, but of the faith of his person before men." Abraham's works merely illustrate the trueness of his faith before people. Leigh presupposes that this verse employs a "similitude"; thus, the real question hinges on the meaning of the key terms relating to the similitude: *body, spirit* or *breath, faith,* and *works.* Leigh suggests that James refers either to "the habit of faith, or . . . the profession of it." The Puritans employed the phrase "habit of faith" (*habitus fidei*) as a technical term to denote "the God-given spiritual capacity of fallen human beings to have faith." In this way, the habit of faith implies a real faith, whereas a professed faith does not. Or, to continue the analogy James uses, the former means that real faith is actually dead faith without works; the latter means that a profession of faith has no value "without a godly life."

Thomas Manton (1620–77)

Thomas Manton was privy to each of the different arguments surrounding the doctrine of justification as well as to the interpretive insights of previous commentators on the Letter of James on 2:14–26, most specifically his Puritan counterparts. The above discussion has been important to illustrate that Manton, like his Puritan colleagues, will interpret this passage according to the analogy of faith. He refers to the controversies surrounding this doctrine in the preface to his commentary:

> For the great controversy of justification, I have handled it as largely as the epistle would give leave. . . . Had I been

aware of some controversies grown since amongst us, I should have said more; yet, take it altogether, enough is said as to my sense, and for vindicating this epistle.

Clearly, James 2:14–26 is a critical section in Manton's commentary.

In conformity with many of his predecessors, Manton divides James 2 into separate sections:

> This chapter contains two special admonitions, which were very needful as the state of things were then. The first is against "respect of persons," because of outward advantages, especially in church matters. The other is against a vain opinion and ostentation of faith, where there was no presence or testimony of works to commend it. James deals in the former admonition from the 1st verse to the 14th. And in the latter from thence to the end of the chapter.

Manton begins his exegesis of this second section by reiterating the scope of this passage. James

> had spoken of a law of liberty; now, lest this expression should justify the misprision of some false hypocrites, who thought they might live as the list, so as they did profess faith in Christ, he disproves the vanity of this conceit by diverse arguments.

From the scope of the passage Manton goes on to expound the passage verse by verse—or, more properly, phrase by phrase within each verse—with accompanying "observations" and "uses."

The first of Manton's comments emerge in relation to the pivotal phrase "If someone says he has faith." Here Manton follows Calvin exactly by explaining that James "does not say 'if any man has faith,' but 'if any man *says* he has faith.'" Manton further sets the tone of the passage by arguing that:

> In this whole discourse the apostle's intent is to show, not *what justifies*, but *who is justified*; not what faith *does*, but what faith *is*. And the drift of the context is not to show that faith without works does not justify, but that a persuasion or assent without works is not faith; and the justification he speaks of is not so much of the person as of the faith.

This important comment sets the tone of the passage because it defuses the controversy surrounding this text. Because James speaks not of true faith but a false one, there is no discrepancy between Paul and James on justification. This situates Manton within the overall Puritan tradition, which takes as its primary focus the reconciliation of Paul and James. Thus far each commentator in this chapter has reconciled the two, with varying degrees of overlap. Whereas Mayer offered double meanings of the terms "faith" and "works," Leigh stressed the difference between justification *coram Deo* ("before God") and justification *coram hominibus* ("before humanity"). Manton offers a combination of the two, perhaps united more closely with Leigh, but with more commentary and a more antagonistic posture. Manton's antagonism is embodied in his anti-Roman rhetoric, which is another hallmark feature of Puritan theology at this time: "It is the folly of the Papists to restrain [works] to acts of charity. There are other products of faith." Throughout this section he takes a defensive position against the Roman Catholic view of justification, just as he will against other unorthodox Protestant views.

After defusing the controversy of the passage in his initial comments on the first verse in this section, Manton comments on the next two verses together. One of the standard interpretations of this passage argues that these verses represent a "similitude" illustrating how a faith without works does not lead to salvation. Manton does not use these exact words, but he understands it as such. He writes that James "compares faith and charity." This reading echoes Calvin's, who likewise makes this comparison. The point of the illustration is to show "that pretences of faith avail no more than pretences of charity."

Manton appeals to verse 19 as confirmation of his overall interpretation that James speaks of a false faith rather than a true one (which is the complete opposite of the Roman Catholic position).

> This instance shows what faith he disputes against, namely, such as consists in bare speculation and knowledge; which can no more save a man than looking on the sun can translate a man into the sphere and orb of it.

Of Manton's four "observations" arising from this verse, only the first merits attention. He writes, "True faith unites to Christ, it is conversant about his person; it is not only *assensus axiomati*, 'an assent to a gospel-maxim' or proposition; you are not justified by that, but by being one with Christ." Manton clearly anchors the doctrine of justification in Christ. As he stated earlier, mere belief in God or in God's promises proves nothing; even the devils believe in God. The person of Christ distinguishes true faith from false faith:

> It was the mistake of the former age to make the promise rather than the person of Christ to be the formal object of faith; the promise is the *warrant*, Christ the *object*: therefore the work of faith is terminated . . . in short, there is not only *assent* in faith, but *consent*; not only an assent to the truth of the word, but a consent to take Christ.

Manton's use of "observations" and "uses" allows him to address specific topics that move beyond the text itself. Thus, in the context of the discussion above, it allows Manton to expand on the Christological component to justification, which James does not expressly mention. This represents an application of the analogy of Scripture from Paul's Letter to the Romans.

Manton then moves his discussion to the most troublesome passage in the entire Letter of James, namely, 2:24. This is for Manton the heart of the passage. Manton writes after citing the verse:

> But you will say, is not this contrary to scripture? . . . How shall we reconcile this difference? I shall not enter upon the main question till I come to the 24th verse; only, for the clearing of the present doubt, give me leave to return something by way of answer.

Thereafter Manton posits two acceptable interpretations of this passage in light of Paul's words to the contrary. The first line of interpretation represents the traditional view in the Puritan exegetical tradition, as attested by each of the commentators surveyed in this chapter: Paul speaks of justification *in foro divino*, while James refers to justification *in foro humano*:

> Well, then, according to this opinion, these two places may be thus reconciled: Paul speaks of the use and office of faith *in foro divino*, before God, and James speaks of the effects and qualities of faith by which it is justified before men.

Manton does not like this reading, and so offers an alternative:

> *Found faithful* is a phrase equivalent to that which James uses, "was justified." Therefore Paul and James may be thus reconciled: Paul speaks of the justifying of a sinner from the curse of his natural condition, the occupations

of the law, etc., and accepting him into the favour of God, which is of grace, and not of debt; James of the justifying and approbation of that faith by which we are thus accepted with God. God gives us the comfort of our former justification by such experiences and fruits of faith, for in them we are found faithful; that is, before God and man approved to have a right faith.

Although this reading differs slightly from the former position, it is important to note that Manton's primary concern lies in reconciling Paul and James. The difference between the two views is subtle. The justification of which Paul speaks concerns the removing of sin and the transference from a state of nature to a state of grace, whereas James discusses the consequences of a person in the state of grace, namely, that he or she will necessarily produce fruits.

Conclusion: The Puritans and the Analogy of Faith

The exegesis of James 2:14–26 among the Puritans in general and Manton in particular centers on two interrelated themes: (i) the analogy of faith (or, more broadly, the analogy of Scripture) and (ii) scope, which allowed for the reconciliation of Paul and James. These are hermeneutical and exegetical issues respectively. Each of the three commentators discussed above not only considered these themes throughout their exegesis, they focused their entire expositions on them.

First, the analogy of faith became a cardinal doctrine within Puritan exegesis. This is especially apparent in troublesome passages like James 2:14–26. As Knapp observes in regard to seventeenth-century exegesis,

the analogy of faith restricted the range of possible meanings which the exegete would consider—other potential meanings of a passage were simply not mentioned since they were excluded a priori by the *analogia fidei* ("analogy of faith") assumption.

This mind-set characterizes the exegesis of James 2:14–26 among the Puritan commentators on the Letter of James. The doctrine of justification by faith alone was, as Luther once stated, the article upon which the church stands or falls. As such, no other part of Scripture could contradict it.

Second, the primary way to interpret James 2:14–26 in accordance with the analogy of faith was by carefully noting the scope of both James and Paul. According to the Puritan exegetes, the error of the early Lutherans, Roman Catholics, Arminians, and Socinians was their failure to correctly identify the scope of the letters by these apostles, thereby hindering a proper reconciliation of Romans with James. In other words, these traditions did not properly adhere to the principle of the analogy of Scripture. Rather than appealing to the biblical canon itself, they appealed to another authority—whether reason or tradition. The Puritans, by contrast, appealed directly to Scripture, and thus interpreted James in light of Paul in a way that reconciled the two according to the analogy of faith. Puritan exegetes believed that the scope of Romans was justification. The scope of James therefore was not justification—at least not justification "before God." Accordingly, James and Paul agree. The Puritan basis for the analogy of Scripture lies in its presuppositions about God and the Bible, included here in the form of a syllogism:

1. God cannot lie, deceive, or be self-contradictory.
2. Scripture is God-breathed or divine.
3. Thus Scripture can neither deceive nor contain contradictions.

Each of the Puritan exegetes examined above, Manton of course included, reconciled Paul and James—however explicitly—according to the analogy of Scripture. These commentators accomplished this either by subsuming their exegesis of James 2:14–26 under its *scopus* ("scope") or according to a certain proposition or argument. John Mayer largely argues that, although James uses the words "faith" and "works" just as Paul does, James uses them in different ways. Edward Leigh maintains that James speaks of a barren faith, whereas Paul speaks of a true one. Thomas Manton asserts that the justification of which Paul speaks concerns the removing of sin and the transference from a state of nature to a state of grace, whereas James discusses the consequences of a person in the state of grace, namely, that he or she will necessarily produce fruits. More importantly, each of these Puritan interpreters is forced to reconcile James with Paul, since they presuppose that the overall scope of Romans is justification; therefore, the scope of James is either something else or a different component to this doctrine. This mind-set can be formulated as follows:

1. The analogy of faith determines that Scripture coheres (and accords with the fundamental articles of faith).
2. Apparent discrepancies in Scripture are to be resolved not simply theologically but exegetically—by noting the scope, drift, proposition, argument, or general point of each book and each section.
3. The scope of Romans is justification.
4. The scope of James is not justification (but rather a false faith, or something else).
5. Thus Paul and James do not contradict each other.

Despite the Puritans' sharp disagreement with Luther over the canonicity of James and the German reformer's use of "scope" due to their differing methodologies, they nevertheless fully agreed with him that Paul's Letter to the Romans is the lens through which to interpret James. Justification is by faith and not by works, in other words, and Paul's clear words on the subject determined the interpretation of James's less clear (or divergent) words. For Manton (and the rest of the Puritans), this is exactly as it should be for two reasons. First, the Epistle of James is a great letter, but Paul's Epistle to the Romans takes precedence, since its "scope" focuses on the most central theme of the Bible, namely, the doctrine of salvation (specifically, salvation by faith and not by works). Second, and equally important, Luther's error of downgrading James has to be corrected. For although Romans is theologically prior to James, it is not canonically privileged, since the Puritans believed that all of the New Testament writings were equally inspired by God.

6

MANTON AND THE ANGLICANS ON JAMES 5:14–16: SETTLING THE SACRAMENTS

James 5:14–16 was put to particularly heavy use in heated debates among Protestant divines [in the seventeenth century].
Luke Timothy Johnson

This scripture [James 5:14] has occasioned much controversy. . . . Popish anointing, or extreme unction, is a mere hypocritical pageantry. . . . This clause [James 5:16] has been diversely applied. The Papists make it the ground of auricular confession, but absurdly.[1]
Thomas Manton

[Puritans] . . . suffered the fate of all those who lose: as they did not control the writing of history, so they were either written out of that history or . . . dismissed variously as [possessing] . . . no intellectual merit whatsoever.
Carl Trueman

1. Extreme unction is the ritual anointing of a sick person, usually near death, by a priest in the Catholic Church; auricular confession is a (private) confession to a priest who absolves the person's sin.

Introduction

When parish priest Thomas Teackle died in 1696, his library in Accomack County, Virginia consisted of more than 300 titles. It represented the second-largest library in the British colonies; only Cotton and Increase Mather possessed more books. Each of their libraries—the Mathers' and Teackle's—contained titles covering diverse subjects. When it came to exegetical works, each shared a common title: Thomas Manton's commentary on James. The fact that Manton's most respected published commentary had sailed across the Atlantic and was used by British colonists raises an important question relating to Puritanism: To what extent did subsequent pastors and teachers make use of a quintessential Puritan biblical commentator like Thomas Manton?

6.1. Map of Virginia in the seventeenth century, where the Teackles lived.

This chapter reveals that only so-called Puritan interpreters made use of Manton's commentary on James after its publication record in the 1650s. Indeed, as Carl Trueman's quote above attests, many Puritans like Manton were effectively "written out of [English] history" subsequent to the Restoration (1660). Although other factors were involved, Manton's commentary on James was mostly confined to Puritan use after its publication.

As has been indirectly noted in the two previous chapters, very few English interpreters wrote extensive commentaries on James during this time period—most were brief annotations. This chapter puts Manton's commentary on James in direct conversation with its later Anglican counterparts in order to illustrate how important Puritans like Manton lost their public voices after the mid-seventeenth century in England. Specifically, this chapter concludes discussion on Manton's most important and well-known work—his commentary on James—by putting it in conversation with commentaries on James by Manton's Anglican[2] contemporaries Henry Hammond (1605–60) and Daniel Whitby (1638–1726). Their interpretation of James 5:14–16 serves as the focal point of this chapter. The final part of this chapter discusses the marginalization of Puritan figures like Manton subsequent to the Restoration (1660).

Thomas Manton (1620–77)

Thomas Manton's interpretation of this unit in James is best understood as a defense against Roman Catholic interpretations of this passage. Before he even offers his interpretation, Manton notes the "controversy" surrounding this section:

2. In this chapter, *Anglicans* refers to Arminian English theologians and pastors in contrast to Puritans who were Calvinist English theologians and pastors. Before this time (roughly 1660), Anglicans included both viewpoints.

> Though in this exercise I would mainly pursue what is
> practical, yet when a matter lies obvious and fair, like the
> angel in the way of Balaam, it cannot be avoided without
> some dispute and discussion: I shall therefore first open
> the phrases, then clear the controversy, then give you the
> observable notes.

This is neither the first nor the last time a section in James
causes Manton to set aside his argument in order to "clear
[a] controversy." Manton has done this on several occasions
thus far—whether in the introduction, James 2:14–26, or
here in 5:14. It is an important point to note, as it illustrates
well Manton's interpretation of James (and other parts of
the Bible). His basis for doing so in this case rests in the
principle of *sola scriptura* ("Scripture alone"). In contrast to
the Roman Catholic position on the sacrament of extreme
unction—which views this passage in James as biblical support (but not necessarily the basis) of the sacrament—
Manton appeals directly and solely to Scripture as the arbiter.
This mind-set, in fact, appears in the "proposition" to one
of Manton's last sermons (1675), "The Scripture Sufficient
without Unwritten Traditions":

> The Scripture is a sufficient rule of Christian faith, or a
> record of all necessary Christian doctrines, without any
> supplement of unwritten traditions, as containing any neces-
> sary matter of faith, and is thus far sufficient for the decision
> of all controversies.

Manton believes that he can "clear the controversy" surrounding this passage in James 5:14 by simply expounding
the text.

Manton's prefatory comments for this verse foreshadow
how he interprets this passage. He disproves the biblical
basis for—or at least the continued usage of—extreme unc-

tion. After including the standard passages in the New Testament touching on sickness, he proceeds directly to the controversy: "From this . . . the Papists collect that extreme unction is not to be administered but to those that are mortally sick." Before Manton discusses the controversy surrounding this practice at length, though, he first considers the remaining phrases of this verse. He begins with the meaning of the term "elders" [literally, "the presbyters"]. Manton notes the history of the usage of the word and adopts the common view of this term among presbyterians (as opposed to episcopalians). He explains that it

> is given to all the offices and administrations in the church, from the apostle to the deacon; apostles, pastors, teachers, ruling brethren, deacons, are all called *elders*. Principally there is understood that order of elders who are elsewhere called *bishops*, whether ruling or teaching elders, chiefly the latter. In sickness we call in the best helps, and it is to be supposed that the best gifts reside in them who are called to teach in the church; and to add the greater seal to their ministry, and to supply the want of physicians, many of them were endued with the gift of healing.

Manton interprets the term "elders" as men of "great skill" who are "associated in all acts of superiority and government" throughout the various churches at this time. This description of the elders follows John Calvin directly, though Manton never mentions him. As for the meaning of the phrase "anointing him with oil," Manton appeals to the famous Dutch Arminian jurist Hugo Grotius, who explains that oil was "a usual symbol of the divine grace" among the Hebrews. Manton maintains that the oil "was not used as an instrument, but as a symbol of the cure." This becomes Manton's indirect way of criticizing extreme unction, which he regards as a "ridiculous hypocrisy."

"Having opened the phrases," Manton explains after commenting on each phrase of verse 14, "I come now to open the controversy, whether this anointing with oil is a standing ordinance in the church?" This issue piques Manton's interests. He writes:

> The Papists make it a sacrament, which they call the sacrament of extreme unction; others in our days [within the Anglican Church?] would revive it as a standing ordinance for church members, expecting some miraculous cure, therefore I must deal with both. I know that the intricacies of dispute are unpleasant to a vulgar ear; therefore I shall not traverse arguments to and fro, but cut the work short by laying down some propositions, that may prevent both the error of the Papists and the novelism of those that would revive this rite in our days.

It is important to reflect on the question that Manton asks: "whether this anointing with oil be a standing ordinance in the church?" Manton's question is deliberate, and he shows his familiarity with these technical terms. He does not ask whether anointing with oil is a "biblical" ordinance; he inquires whether it is a "standing" ordinance. The nature of Manton's question—along with the way he handles the passage—comes directly from John Calvin's interpretation. Calvin writes:

> So we have no dispute, whether anointing with oil was once a sacrament; but whether it has been given to be so perpetually. This latter we deny, because it is evident that the thing signified has long ago ceased.

Manton follows Calvin exactly by arguing that extreme unction is less a question of biblical precedence and more so of dominical institution (which hearkens back to Martin

Luther in his criticism of the sacrament in *The Babylonian Captivity of the Church* in 1520).

Manton constructs five "propositions" against the view that anointing with oil should be a standing ordinance in the church. First, "In the very apostles' time, when it was most in use, it was not absolutely necessary, nor instituted

6.2. Title page for Luther's *The Babylonian Captivity of the Church*, where he attacks the seven sacraments.

by Christ." Manton concedes that certain Protestants in his day argue that Christ did institute the sacrament as a "temporary rite," but he appeals to Peter Lombard, Thomas Cajetan, and other Catholics who "all found it upon apostolical [and thus not dominical] practice." "For my part," Manton continues, "I think it was only approved by Christ, and not instituted, and taken up as a usual practice among the Hebrews." Manton interprets this practice as God's way of condescending to Israel. Although there is no medicinal value in the oil itself, God allowed the Hebrews to apply it when healing—thus serving as a symbol to the gift of healing. Manton raises additional rhetorical questions about why God would act this way, but he defends God's actions of allowing the custom and the symbol "as long as the gift remained."

Manton's second proposition against the continued ordinance of extreme unction reads:

> In the apostles' time it was promiscuously used and applied to every member of the church, but with great prudence and caution, for the apostles only anointed those of whose recovery they were assured by the Holy Ghost, as James here seems to restrain it to such an object where they could pray in faith. He that gave the gift did always suggest the seasons of using it; with the power he gave discretion, that by a common use they might not expose the gift to scorn.

This common Protestant interpretation indirectly undermines the practice of extreme unction by Roman Catholic priests whom Protestants collectively regarded as misusing or misappropriating "the gift" that God gave only to the apostles or elders in the primitive church. It further undercuts the practice since priests administered the sacrament of extreme unction to those at the point of death; Puritans discerned no such last rite in James's words.

The third proposition Manton gives in opposition to maintaining the ordinance relates to the Protestant view, which states, "In the more common use of [the gift] afterward, all were not healed that were anointed." This argument contains two points. The first is that the ordinance "did not depend upon anointing, but the prayer of faith." Once again, Manton follows Calvin here. As Calvin explains:

> As James brings before us this special gift, to which the external rite was an addition, we hence learn, that the oil could not have been rightly used without faith. But since it appears that the Papists have no certainty as to their anointing, as it is manifest that they have not the gift, it is evident that their anointing is spurious.

In the estimation of Protestants, Roman Catholics ultimately disregarded the center of the entire ordinance: prayer. Whereas Roman Catholics administered extreme unction to those at the point of death—and not with the intention of physical healing—Protestants like Manton argued that faith was meant to restore physically the health of the one sick. This leads to the second point. Because this practice was successful during apostolic times, the mere fact that it is no longer successful—that is, people no longer recover from their sickness upon receiving the sacrament—proves that it is not a perpetual ordinance within the church.

The fourth proposition relates to the third:

> When [the gift of healing] did cease we cannot tell; when it should cease we may easily judge, if we will but understand the nature, use, and end.

The Protestant doctrine of the cessation of spiritual gifts originates, in part, in reaction to the sacrament of extreme unction. Beginning no later than Calvin, each Protestant interpreter before Manton argued that spiritual gifts no longer function. The gifts ceased during the apostolic era— by at least the second century. As Manton states it, "The rite ceased when the gift ceased, which God has taken from the world almost these fifteen hundred years." Manton next relays the popular story that the church father Tertullian told about a Christian named Proculus who apparently anointed Emperor Severus with oil and cured him from sickness. If this story is true—and Manton deems it apocryphal—then the gift of healing continued, at least sporadically, until the third century.

Manton's fifth proposition against the continued ordinance of anointing the sick with oil serves as the conclusion: "Popish anointing, or extreme unction, is a mere hypocritical pageantry." This represents the collective opinion of Protestants. In the words of John Calvin, the Roman Catholic practice of extreme unction is "spurious"; the Danish Lutheran Niels Hemmingsen asserts that it expedites "their dead to be sent into hell"; the preacher John Mayer calls it "a bare ceremony without operation"; while parliamentary colonel Edward Leigh refers to it as "a vain superstitious imitation." Manton is the heir to this Protestant interpretive tradition, and he differs from his predecessors only by arrangement of argument, not in substance. He concludes his fifth proposition by belittling the meticulousness and detail of the administration of the sacrament.

Of Manton's six observations or practical applications of the passage that arise from this verse, the fifth is noteworthy. He writes that "sins are often the cause of sickness." This is another standard view in Protestant exegesis of this passage, which suggests that the Roman Catholic practice of extreme unction deals insufficiently with the real problem, which is sin. By arguing that sin causes physical sickness, the Protestants turn the focus from the sacrament to prayer, that is, from an external rite to an inward morality.

Manton's discussion of sin and sickness allows him to discuss the doctrine of inherent sin, namely, that it is the fallen condition of humankind to remain in sin throughout life. Christ alone takes away this sin. "In taking away sickness, which is the effect, Christ would represent taking away sin, which is the cause; Christ's act in taking away sickness was a type of taking away sin." Sin causes sickness, and Christ's physical healing in the Gospels is a type of his removal of sin at the cross and through his resurrection.

Manton's discussion of verse 16 resumes his discussion of the sacraments. He comments on the phrase "Confess your faults one to another." After noting the Greek terms, he states that this verse "has been diversely applied." He has in mind, of course, the Roman Catholic interpretation of this verse: "The Papists make it the ground of auricular confession, but absurdly." Manton's work stands in a long line of Protestant exegesis of this passage, all of which strongly opposed auricular confession. Manton makes use of all of these interpretive insights, and his defensive posture is once again notable. Before getting into the controversy, however, Manton explains the interpretive options.

The first, the traditional Roman Catholic view, Manton rejects on the grounds that "the priest must as well confess to the penitent person, as the penitent person to the priest," since James implies a "reciprocal" confession. Manton echoes Calvin's view. As the Genevan reformer explains,

> For since a mutual, or to speak plainly, a reciprocal confession is demanded here, no others are bidden to confess their own sins, but those who in their turn are fit to hear confession of others.

This is Calvin's clever way of turning the sacrament of auricular confession on its head, and Manton uses it accordingly. This view, Manton continues, precedes Calvin and is actually found in certain Roman Catholic interpreters who have altogether abandoned this text as biblical support for auricular confession.

Finally, Manton refers to two other possible views in regard to this passage, both of which he rejects: the interpretation that James speaks of injuries done to others; and, similarly, that James speaks of sins of "joint consent," by which Manton means mutual sins such as lust between a man and a woman. Manton breaks down this phrase into one overall observation, which contains several parts. The observation is: "there is a season of confessing our sins, not only to God, but to man." Here Manton is clearly reacting to the opposing view. Just as he stated earlier in regard to justification, Protestants are opposed to neither good works nor confession to God and others. However, a clear difference between Protestants and Roman Catholics emerges. Manton explains, "I will not digress into controversy [which is not really true, as he does just that here]; I shall briefly show—(1.) The evils and inconveniences of that confession which the Papists require; (2.) The seasons wherein we must confess to man."

First, Manton describes the practice of auricular confession.

> The Papists call it the sacrament of penance, by which a man is bound, at least once a year, to confess to a priest all the sins he has committed since he was last shriven, with all the circumstances of it, *quis* [who], *quid* [what], *ubi* [where], *quibus auxiliis* [with what], etc.

Here, echoing the phrases delineated by the Fourth Lateran Council (1215), Manton seeks only to demonstrate the pointlessness of this practice. He offers four counterarguments:

1. he disapproves of the "absolute necessity of it; confession to men being a thing only necessary in some cases; in others confession to God may be enough";
2. "this scrupulous enumeration is nothing else but a rack of conscience, invented and exercised without any reason";
3. Manton detests that the Roman Catholic Church makes this sacrament "of divine institution." He then advances the common Protestant complaint that this sacrament was invented in the thirteenth century by Innocent the Third; and
4. this Catholic sacrament "is tyrannical, dangerous to the security and peace of princes, betraying their counsels, infamous and hazardous to all men."

Second, after using logic to demonstrate the fallacy of the Roman Catholic sacrament of confession, Manton then describes the proper means of confessing. This occurs in two ways: confession before God and before others. Manton explains, "We are not against all confession, as the Papists slander us." Although this statement represents a common Protestant complaint, Manton broadens the exegetical tradition of this verse by detailing the acceptable means of confession. Manton divides confession into public and private confession, both of which occur—though on different occasions—before God and before others.

Henry Hammond (1605–60)

Henry Hammond originally wrote his annotations on James in 1653, a mere two years after Manton published his

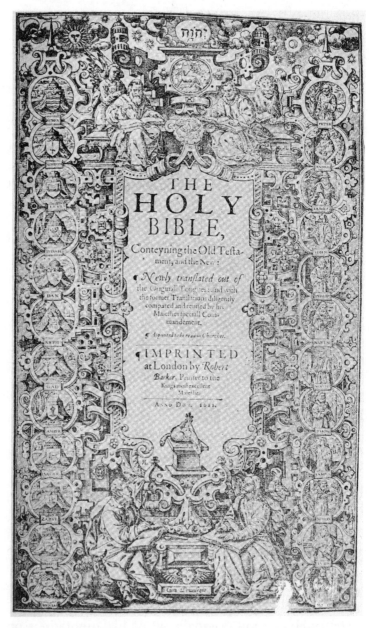

6.3. Title page of the Authorized Version (KJV), which was used by countless theologians like Hammond.

commentary. A priest in the Church of England, Hammond was educated at Magdalen Hall, Oxford (BA, 1622; MA, 1625) and wrote several works before receiving an invitation to be personal chaplain to Charles I. Hammond was a noted episcopalian and royalist who was closely watched during the Interregnum. He composed his paraphrases and annotations on the entire New Testament while confined at Oxford, which was the headquarters to the royalist camp where Charles I resided during the First Civil War in the early and mid-1640s. This impressive exegetical work was catered to the popular demand for English biblical expositions.

Hammond's paraphrase and annotations went through several editions. As scholar Richard Muller explains:

> Beyond the strictly "Reformed" works, but highly significant in the exegetical and doctrinal discussions of the era, are Hammond's *Paraphrase and Annotations* on the New Testament and Grotius' annotations on the Old and New Testaments, both of which evidence a similar combination of textual with topical annotation.

Muller rightly notes the similarities between Hugo Grotius and Henry Hammond, for not only did Hammond compose his work on the basis of Grotius's, but the royalist also defended the Dutchman's theological orthodoxy on more than one occasion.

Hammond's paraphrase and annotations contain three parts: the King James Version of the New Testament, his paraphrase, and his annotations. His discussion of James 5:14–16 is thus not distinguished from the rest of the fifth chapter. There are, at once, several similarities and differences between Hammond's exegesis of 5:14 and Manton's. First, Hammond explicitly links sin with physical sickness. Whereas Manton more cautiously asserts that sin is oftentimes the cause of physical sickness, Hammond directly states that the person mentioned in James is sick because he committed a sin "either against God or man." It is for this reason, secondly, that Hammond and Manton both stress the need for the person to appeal to the elders.

However, they differ widely in their understandings of the role of the elders. For Manton, the principal role of the elders is to pray for the person who is sick; the effects of their faithful prayers strengthen the sick person both physically and spiritually. For Hammond, by contrast, the elders are properly "Bishops," not simply godly men in the congregation. This, of course, directly opposes Manton's presbyterian understanding of the term "elder" and illustrates the difference between Manton the Puritan and Hammond the Anglican. Hammond views it as the function of the bishops to anoint the sick person with oil, hear his confession, and pray to God for his physical and spiritual restoration. Next, Hammond and Manton equally oppose the Roman Catholic sacrament of extreme unction. Their reasons are similar: Jesus did not command the use of this sacrament, the purpose of anointing with oil is (physical and spiritual) healing, and spiritual gifts are no longer operative in the church.

Hammond's interpretation of verse 15 largely extends the similarities and differences that exist between him and Manton. In his paraphrase of this verse Hammond translates the Greek word for *presbyter* as "bishop" rather than "presbyter." In terms of church government, this certainly reflects his support of episcopalianism rather than (Manton's) presbyterianism. In the seventeenth century commentators put the epistles of church fathers Ignatius and Polycarp to heavy use regarding the ecclesiology of the early church. Hammond made use of and defended the episcopal positions of these early letters. Manton, of course, was an ardent champion of presbyterianism, and he had dedicated much of his midcareer to the establishment of this form of government around London in the 1640s and 1650s. Although Manton and his friend Richard Baxter were willing to compromise on this matter in the early 1660s by adopting James Usher's plea for reduced episcopacy in order to secure comprehension within the Church of England, their attempts failed entirely.

Hammond's interpretation of verse 16 mostly concerns itself with issues related to language. In his paraphrase Hammond continues his interpretation of the two previous verses that the sick person should confess his sins to the bishop whose fervent prayer will both impact the sick person and ascend to God who will either answer the bishop's prayer or not. Here Hammond agrees with Manton. In his annotations Hammond devotes the entire discussion to philological and textual issues with the intention of more firmly grounding his conclusion, namely, that the sick person is to confess to a bishop and not any ordinary person. However, Hammond differs from Manton in his interpretation of this verse theologically. Hammond argues that the confession James refers to in this passage exists between an inferior (the sick person) and a superior (the bishop). He constructs this argument on the basis of the Greek text, which he avers "must signify, as it is defined by the matter, subjection which is not mutual." Manton, for his part, argued exactly the opposite: The confession described here is mutual; in this way he seeks to completely deconstruct the sacrament of auricular confession.

Daniel Whitby (1638–1726)

Daniel Whitby was a clergyman in the Church of England and most active subsequent to the Restoration in 1660, when the monarchy was restored and the Anglican Church forced out its Puritan remnant. He attended Trinity College, Oxford (BA, 1657; MA, 1660; BD and DD, 1672) and held the living at St. Edmund's until his death. Whitby was a controversialist who spent much of his life publishing polemical works on diverse topics. He was strongly anti-Catholic as well as an ardent Arminian, and he was especially known for his knowledge of the Greek Fathers. During the late 1690s he dedicated his time to writing a commentary on the entire New Testament, of which the epistles were first published in 1700 (and the complete New Testament in 1703). This work was considered a classic in the eighteenth century and went through several printings.

Whitby's work on James is both more combative and more scholastic in design than Hammond's commentary. In this way, it resembles Manton's. Whitby divides the section on James 5:14–16 into two major sections: a translation of the Greek text and his notes and accompanying arguments arising from the text. Whitby's annotations on the first phrase of verse 14 provide an eclectic overview of several different interpretations. Whitby parallels Manton by translating "presbyter" as "elder" rather than "bishop"; but he follows Hammond by interacting with the early Greek Fathers regarding the use of this term; and he, like Richard Baxter before him, argues that "there must be more than one Bishop in the Church of which the sick man is a member."

Whitby's interpretation of the remainder of these two verses shows additional use of the interpretive tradition. Whitby notes the common Jewish practice of anointing and how many Jews during Jesus' time healed the sick by anointing them with oil. He also draws attention to the gift of faith among the elders that enabled them to perform "miraculous and extraordinary" wonders. Whitby, more-over, previously as the author of several treatises against Roman Catholicism, devotes full attention to refuting the sacrament of extreme unction: "Hence it is evident, that there is no foundation for the Sacrament of Extreme Unc-tion." This argument leads Whitby into a scholastic debate with Rome, as embodied in the comments by Frenchman Gulielmus Estius (1542–1613), who, Richard Muller notes, "offered both a masterful literal exegesis and an urbane response to the Protestant interpretation of key texts." Whitby offers five objections and answers to Estius con-cerning miracles—a discussion otherwise unparalleled in the exegetical tradition.

The first objection states that miracles do not extend to "Spiritual Effects, as the Forgiveness of Sins, but Temporal [Effects]." Whitby responds that this contradicts Jesus' prac-tice in the Gospels. The second objection argues that this section in James does not refer to healing as such; otherwise James would have encouraged those with the gift of healing to restore the sick rather than calling upon "the elders." Whitby responds that the elders are called because it is their "Office" to pray over the sick. Third, Estius maintains that this text refers to believers, "whereas the use of Miracles was chiefly for converting Infidels." Whitby counters that Paul was not aware of this sacrament; had he been aware, he would have administered it to those dying, like Epaph-roditus (cf. Philippians 2:27). The fourth objection is, "had the Apostle [James] intended miraculous Healing, Oil [would not have] been prescribed, Christ having said, they *should lay their hands on the sick* only." Whitby contends that "one ceremony excludes not the other." Moreover, he argues that the laying on of hands "is prescribed in Preaching to the *Gentiles*," while anointing with oil is a Jewish practice. Finally, the fifth objection states that "[because] all the other things delivered in this Epistle belong to the *Christians* of all ages, this therefore must do so too." Whitby reasons to the contrary and cites 1 Peter 4:10–11 as evidence that the apostles can speak of both permanent and temporal things together.

This whole discussion rests on two assumptions. The Protestant assumption, as argued by Whitby, is as follows: The practice to which James 5:14–15 refers always resulted in healing; thus, the sacrament of extreme unction, which does not heal the sick, is mistakenly derived from this text. What is more, the gift of healing has ceased. The Roman Catholic assumption, as argued by Estius, is as follows: The discussion in James 5:14–15 does not refer to miraculous healing; thus, the sacrament of extreme unction does not need to heal people in order to be a legitimate practice. The practice James refers to—the practice of calling on elders in the community to pray over the sick—must be continued since there is no agreed criterion for deciding what should be permanent and what should be temporal.

In contrast to his discussion on 5:14–15, Whitby does not include an interpretation of James 5:16. This is surely surprising, as this verse had become the exegetical battleground for or against the sacrament of auricular confession. The Protestants, of course, sought to wrest this text from the Roman Catholics; they appealed both to the plain sense of the text and to reason in support of their interpretation. Given Whitby's strong aversion to all things Roman Catholic and, in particular, his argument with Estius above, one might expect that he would continue this argument against auricular confession. He does not. Aside from his English translation (which parallels the King James Version), he mentions neither auricular confession nor Roman Catholicism. His debate above with Estius serves as the final comments he makes on this section.

Conclusion

Thomas Manton's comments on James 5:14–16 received minimal engagement in England between the years of 1650 and 1700. Neither of the two Anglican interpreters examined in this chapter interacted with Manton. In fact, when compared at all to other commentaries written on James during this time period, Matthew Poole's exhaustive commentary on the Bible is the only work that engages Manton's. Unlike Manton, the two Anglicans—Hammond and Whitby—were on the winning side of the church at this time in England's history, while Puritans like Manton were on the losing side. This illustrates well how Manton's commentary in general and his life and thought in particular had its limits—historically, theologically, and geographically.

Historically, Manton published his commentary on James during the Interregnum and Protectorate (1649–60), when Puritans exercised considerable power politically and theologically. It was during these years that Manton was at the height of his career. At this time he published both of his complete biblical commentaries (on James and Jude); he was a leader in the classis movement around London; he was a chaplain to Oliver Cromwell; he was appointed a Trier; he preached regularly before Parliament; he wrote the preface to the second edition to the Westminster Confession of Faith; he received the rectory at St. Paul's, Covent Garden; he was held in favor by many of the nobility; he received his Doctor of Divinity; and he was appointed a personal chaplain to Charles II upon his restoration in 1660. After this time period, however, the political and theological backlash against Puritans like Manton was swift and severe. Manton lost his living, was involved in fruitless negotiations at comprehension, and was even imprisoned. It is little wonder, therefore, that Manton's biblical commentaries—in this case, on the Epistle of James—found favor only among, from this moment forward, the nonconformist Puritans. The Puritans had lost their public voice.

Theologically, only those in the Puritan tradition incorporated Manton's work into their exegetical tradition. This usage manifests itself in the commentaries of Matthew Poole (1624–79), Matthew Henry (1662–1714), and John Gill (1697–1771). Those outside of the Puritan tradition such as Hammond and Whitby did not engage Manton's commentary. This confirms an important fact: Although Manton drew regularly from diverse traditions outside of his own—whether Roman Catholic, Arminian, or otherwise—only the Puritan tradition made use of his work subsequent to his death.

Geographically, Manton's commentary on James received a better reception in colonial America than in Britain—and certainly not in any other location. Besides the fact that Thomas Teackle and the Mathers owned Manton's work, other important colonial figures such as Jonathan Edwards (1703–58) made use of his commentary. However, because colonial Americans did not publish commentaries on James, this meant that Manton became a forgotten figure. Indeed, the failed reception of Cotton Mather's (1663–1728) "Biblia Americana," which he wrote over the course of two decades before his death but never procured a printer to publish it, generally attests to the fact that colonial Americans did not influence the interpretive tradition. As such, Manton's commentary failed to enter the mainstream biblical tradition among his successors in any way similar to the way he incorporated previous tradition into his commentary on James.

PART THREE

MANTON AS PUBLIC PREACHER: SELECTED SERMONS

Now that the historical circumstances of Thomas Manton's life have been amply described in Part One and his most well-known work (on the Epistle of James) has been thoroughly analyzed in Part Two, this section offers selections of some of Manton's isolated sermons as well as brief introductions to them. The purpose of this section is to familiarize readers with Manton's actual works with only limited remarks, so they will then be able to begin reading Manton's other works on their own afterward. As an author once stated with regard to writing a commentary on a book of the Bible, so too can the case be made for writing a book on Manton: There is a great difference between reading a book about Manton's writings and actually reading Manton's writings. Although the former is foundational, the latter is indispensable.

To help introduce readers to Manton's sermons, this section is divided into three chapters. Each of these chapters contains a brief introduction, with an edited sermon following. Deciding which sermons to choose was no easy matter, but the three chosen are intended to give a different glimpse into Manton's style. One sermon concentrates on one of

Jesus' well-known commands in the Gospels for his disciples to deny themselves; one was delivered in public and focused on a prophetic book in the Old Testament; and another one is an exposition of an obscure verse in the book of Genesis. Each of the sermons has been edited and modernized, but they all clearly retain Manton's own style and phrasing.

Each of the chapters in this section contains a specific focus, with the additional purpose of bringing out a different glimpse of Manton's sermons. Chapter 7 focuses on Manton as a minister, and it contains one of his sermons on the Christian life. Chapter 8 concentrates on Manton as a public figure, and as such it contains an edited sermon that he preached before Parliament. The final chapter in the section, Chapter 9, considers Manton as a preacher and therefore focuses on the main content of his preaching: Jesus Christ and his call for his disciples to live and love like their master.

7

Manton as Minister: Learning How to Meditate

> [Manton's] work . . . is above all "practical," that is, directed to the religious life and practices of his learners; all his learning tends to this end.
> Luke Timothy Johnson

> [T]he Puritans insisted that the preachers' task is to feed their congregations with the contents of the Bible—not the dry husks of their own fancy, but the life-giving word of God.
> J. I. Packer

Introduction

Thomas Manton's friend and colleague Richard Baxter wrote in his *A Christian Directory* that "Scripture is the glass in which you may see the Ancient of Days, the Eternal Majesty shining in his glory . . . and Christ reigning as the King of all the world." Nevertheless, Baxter continues, each of these great and glorious thoughts become all but "dry and barren" if Christians do not "meditate" properly. In between Manton's role as a public citizen of the English state and a preacher of God's Word stands a man who sought after

7

moral reform. In essentially all of his hundreds of sermons that he preached over the course of thirty-five years, Manton never tired of calling people to mend their ways and to get right with God.

One of the primary ways that Manton encouraged people to do so was by meditating on Scripture. For the Puritans, meditation was the practical companion to something else they did about as well as any other of their time: study. It is well known that Puritans understood study to be one of the primary ways that people worship God. As such, many Puri-

7.1. Portrait of Richard Baxter, a friend and colleague of Manton's.

tan pastors—attempting to worship God without end—often spent entire days alone in their studies. Jonathan Edwards, for instance, rarely concerned himself with pastoral calls while he was minister of the church at Northampton and instead preferred to remain in his study for most of the day. Exceptions to this general rule were made for meditating—when he would travel to a field alone to spend time with God. These twin worshipful acts, meditation and study, were the pillars of a Puritan's devotional life. Manton explains the difference between meditation and study in the following sermon:

> The goal of study is information, but the goal of meditation is practice, or a work upon affections. . . . In study we are rather like vintners, who take in wines to store themselves for sale. In meditation we are like customers who buy wine for our use and comfort. A vintner's cellar may be better stored than a customer's but he has it for others' use. The one who studies may have more of perception and knowledge, and his cellar may be better stocked, but he does not have it for taste and necessary refreshment as the Christian does.

Manton's Sermon on Meditating

In the sermon that follows, Thomas Manton provides a tour de force on why and how Christians should meditate. His purpose in the sermon is straightforward: to convince everyone that meditation is necessary for their right knowledge of God and of themselves.[1] Manton drives home this principle mightily, as the following sermon is merely the first of ten on one tiny verse! How Manton was able to produce ten lengthy and insightful sermons on just one verse is a testimony to his knowledge and imagination as well as

---

1. *The Complete Works of Thomas Manton* (Worthington, PA: Maranatha Publications, 1900), 5:381–409.

to his Puritan upbringing. As is typical of Puritan pastors, the sermon is dense, doctrinal, and deep. The exact date of this sermon is not known.

Sermon on Genesis 24:63

"And Isaac went out to meditate in the field at the evening." (Gen. 24:63)

The context of this passage describes the journey of Rebekah with Abraham's servant, and the text shows the occasion of the first conversation between Isaac and Rebekah. Isaac goes out into the fields to meditate, and suddenly he sees the camels coming.

I cannot pass by this accident without some remark and observation. Isaac goes to meet with God, and he ends up meeting with Rebekah in addition to God. Godliness has the promises of this life and that which is to come; there is nothing lost by duty and acts of piety and worship. Seneca said the Jews were an unhappy people because they lost the seventh part of their lives, by which he means the time they spent resting on the Sabbath. This is the logic of nature, to think that all bestowed on God is lost. Flesh and blood snuffs and cries, "What weariness is it, and why do we need all this waste?" Oh, let me tell you: By serving God you drive on two cares at once. Worldly interests many times are cast into the way of religion, and, besides the main design, these things are added to us. Wonderful are the providences of God in and about duties of worship. Some have gone aside to pray, and escaped such as lay in wait to destroy them; and Martin Luther tells a story of one who balked a duty and fell into a danger, passed by a sermon, and was presently surprised by thieves. There are others who thought of nothing but meeting God in his worship, and God has made their duties an occasion of advancing their outward comforts. Certainly it is good to obey all impulses of the Spirit; there may be providence as well as grace in it: "Isaac went out to meditate in the field at the evening; and he lifted up his eyes and saw that the camels were coming."

In the words you have several circumstances:

1. The person: "Isaac."
2. His work: "He went out to meditate."
3. The place: "in the field."
4. The time: "at the evening."

1. For the person, Isaac. I need not say much, since I do not want to digress. He was Abraham's son, and God said of Abraham, "I know him, that he will command his children, and his household after him, and they shall keep the way of the Lord, to do justice and judgment." Good education leaves a savor and dye upon the spirit, at least an awe and a care of duties and exercises of religion; and therefore it is no wonder to hear of Abraham's son who had been trained up in the way of the Lord, to go out to meditate; it is a seal of the blessing of education. Isaac was now in his youth; certainly he could not be very old. Sarah was ninety years old when the promise was first made to her of a son, but 127 years old when she died. And this incident was immediately after her death, for just as Isaac received Rebekah he left off his mourning for Sarah. Probably Isaac was now a little above thirty.

Isaac, a young man who was now entering into the world, goes out to meditate. Usually we make religious exercises the work of older people, and after we have spent the heat and flower of our spirits in the vanities of the world, we hope to make amends for all by a severe and devout retirement.

Younger people look upon meditation as a dull, melancholy work, fit only for the phlegm and decay of old age; vigorous and eager spirits are more for action than thoughts, and their work lies so much with others that they have no time to descend into themselves. But the elder world was more innocent; the exercises of Isaac's youth were pious; he went out into the field to meditate.

2. To open his work to you, "to meditate," or, as it is in the margin, "to pray." This word properly signifies muttering, or an imperfect and suppressed sound. The Greek Old Testament (Septuagint) sometimes renders it by "to sing," but here it signifies "to exercise himself." It is most properly a sports exercise, as if his going out had been only for sport and to enjoy himself after the toil of the day. But that is not so probable; the Holy Spirit would not put such a mark upon such a circumstance. Therefore I suppose the Septuagint's word must be taken more largely to comprise also a religious exercise. But which is it, to pray or meditate? I would not depart from our own Hebrew translation without weighty cause; most other translations look that way. Symmachus renders it "to speak"; Aquila, "to discourse as with others," that is, with God and his own soul. And so it suits with the force of the original word, which properly signifies to mutter, or such a speaking as is between thoughts and words. In this way, the meaning is that he went aside privately to discourse with God about God's promises and about heavenly things.

3. The place, "in the field." Partly for privacy, deep thoughts require solitude. Many of David's psalms were penned in the wilderness. He who would have the company of God and his own thoughts must go aside from other company and be alone that he may not be alone, that the mind, being sequestered from all distractions, may solace itself the more freely in these heavenly thoughts: "Moses led the flock to

the backside of the desert and came to the mountain of God, even to Horeb." He goes aside from the other shepherds, so that he might converse with the great shepherd and bishop of our souls, and there he sees the vision of the burning bush. When God communicates his love to the church, he invites her into the wilderness: "Behold, I will allure her, and bring her into the wilderness, and speak comfortably to her." The most familiar and intimate conversations between God and the church are in private. So the spouse invites the bridegroom: "Come, my beloved, let us go forth into the field, let us lodge in the villages." In these solitary and heavenly retreats to which no eyes are conscious and privy, we most experience God and ourselves. Duties done in company are easier; the eyes of others may have an influence upon our worship; and therefore meditation is difficult and tedious, because it is a work of being alone, which has approval from none but our Father who sees in secret. Partly because the field is an aid to meditation, fancy and invention being elevated and raised by the sweetness, variety, and pleasure of it, there are on every side so many objects and lively memorials of God. However, in this sense the circumstance is not binding. Some do better in a room than in a field or garden, where the senses—being locked from all other objects—allows the mind to fall more directly upon itself, which otherwise in a field or garden would skip from object to object, without focusing upon any seriously.

4. The last circumstance in the text is the time, "at the evening," which is also a matter of an arbitrary concern. Time in itself is but an inactive circumstance. All hours are alike to God; he takes no more pleasure in the sixth or ninth hour than in the first hour. What matters is that you should prudently observe when your spirit is most fresh and alert. To some the morning is best, when it seems most fit to offer spiritual and heavenly thoughts, before the mind receives

any images and thoughts from outside fleshly objects. Morning thoughts are, as it were, virgin thoughts of the mind, before they have been prostituted to these inferior and baser objects, and so are more pure and sublime; and then the soul, like the hind of the morning, with a swift and nimble readiness climbs up to the mountain of myrrh and to the hill of frankincense: "Until the day breaks and the shadows flee away, I will go to the mountain of myrrh and to the hill of frankincense." And it tends much to season the whole day when we can talk with the law in the morning: "When you awake, it shall talk with you."

To some the evening seems more appropriate—that when the vanity of the spirit has been spent in business, their thoughts may be more serious and solemn with God. And after the weights have been running down all day through their busyness in the world, they may wind them up again at night in these recesses and exercises of piety and religion. As David says, "Unto you, O Lord, I lift up my soul."

To others the silence and stillness of the night seems to be a help; and because of the curtain of darkness that is drawn between them and the world, they can better entertain serious and solemn thoughts of God. David speaks everywhere in the psalms of his night devotions: "When I remember you upon my bed, and meditate on you in the night-watches." The expression is taken from the custom of the Jews, who divided the night into many watches. While others were resting their bodies on their beds, David was resting his soul in the bosom of God, and he gives less rest to his eyes so that he might give the more to his soul. "My eyes prevent the night-watches, so that I might meditate in your word." Certainly in the night, when we are taken off from other business, we have the greatest command of our thoughts; and the cover of darkness that God has stretched over the world begets a greater awe and reverence. Therefore, it is told that one person, when he pressed any weighty point and perceived any who did not care, used to beg of them that if God by his providence should suffer them to awake in the night, they would think of his words. Certainly the mind, being by sleep emptied of other cares, like a mill falls upon itself, and the natural awe and terror which is the effect of darkness helps to make the thoughts more solemn and serious. So, you see that much may be said for the convenience of either of these seasons, evening or morning, or night. It is your duty to be faithful to your own souls, and sometimes to take the advantage either of the night or of the day, or the morning, or the evening as best suits us. David says, "Oh, how I love your law! It is my meditation all the day." So he describes this blessed person: "His delight is in the law of the Lord, and in his law he meditates day and night," that is, sometimes in the day and sometimes in the night; no time can come amiss to a prepared spirit.

But Isaac's hour was in the evening; in the evening he went out to meditate, in which two things are notable. Firstly, that he made his obligation to commune with God his refreshment. Isaac had worked all day, and in the evening he goes to refresh himself with God. What a shame it is that what was Isaac's solace is our burden! If we had spiritual discernment, we should soon see that there is no delight like that of the duty of communing with God, and no refreshment like that which we enjoy in the exercises of religion and in communion with God. The world's delights are vain; they may provoke amusement, but they cannot yield any pure, solid, and true contentment. It was Christ's meat to do his Father's will: "My meat is to do the will of him who sent me, and to finish his work." It was sweeter to Job to hear God's word than to have his appointed food: "I have esteemed the words of his mouth more than my necessary food." And David says, "Your statutes have been my songs in the house of my pilgrimage." All the comfort he had to drive away the sad and disconsolate hours of his pilgrimage was to exercise himself in the study and meditation of God's word. And it was Isaac's evening comfort to go out and meditate. Gracious hearts must have spiritual delights: the word and obedience and prayer and meditation. As one said, "Either this is not the gospel, or we are not Christians!" Either these histories are not true, or our hearts are much unlike theirs. Oh, how sweet it would be if we could make our obligation our recreation, and our work our pleasure; that after a full day's work we would take a turn with God in the mountain and walk in the garden of love. As David said, "My meditation of him will be sweet; I will be glad in the Lord." Isaac went out in the evening.

Secondly, that at the evening his spirit was still fresh and savory. This was the time not of necessity but of choice. Many spend their energy and strength in the world, toiling all day, and in the evening come and offer God a drowsy, yawning prayer, when all the vigor of their spirits is wasted. You should bring forth the best wine last; never so engage in the world as to hinder an obligation. It should be the wisdom of Christians to guide their affairs with such judgment that duties may not become burdensome and wearisome. Now a soul encumbered with business cannot act with such delight and freedom as it ought. We too often suffer the lean part rather than enjoying the fat part. Mary has cause to complain of Martha; so much time is spent in the world that we have no heart or strength for communion with God. And finally when all are asleep and wearied out with the world, then we call to duty. Oh, remember in the evening and at the close of the day that your affections should be quick and free for spiritual things. Isaac went out in the evening.

I shall sum up the intent of the whole verse in this one point:

Doctrine: It is the duty of Christians to dedicate and set apart some time and place for solemn meditation, or the exercising of their souls on heavenly and holy things.

My purpose is to speak of meditation, a duty unaccustomed and unpracticed. Both the practice and the knowledge of it are strangers to us. The times are times of action and tumult, and we all think that we have so much to do with others that few desire to converse with God and themselves. Our case is somewhat like those in Nehemiah's time: "With one hand they wrought in the work, and with the other hand held a weapon." We are forced to fight and quarrel for our religion, that we may rescue the innocent and holy principles of it from violation and scorn. I observe that many Christians use the sword; they spend the heat and strength of their spirits in controversies. But I doubt that they use the trowel enough, and they are not as earnest in private devotions as they are in public. Therefore I shall make it my work to press the duty of meditation.

My method shall be this: I shall show:

1. What meditation is.
2. The necessity and profit of it.
3. The rules that serve to guide us in the holy work and business.
4. The lets and hindrances of it, with the helps and remedies against them.
5. The object or matters upon which you are to meditate, which I shall handle first, generally, and secondly, particularly.

I shall give you some hints of meditation on those objects which are most usual and most practical. 1. What meditation is. Before I can define it I must distinguish it. Firstly, there is that which we call occasional meditation, which is an act by which the soul spiritualizes every object about which it is conversant.

A gracious heart is like a distilling or purifying instrument that can filter useful meditations out of all things with which it meets. As it sees all things in God, so it sees God in all things. Our Lord at the well discourses of "the water of life." At dinner with the Pharisee, one discourses of "eating bread in the kingdom of God." There is a chemistry and holy art that a Christian has to turn water into wine, brass into gold—to make earthly occasions and objects to minister spiritual and heavenly thoughts. God trained up the old church by types and ceremonies, that upon a common object they might ascend to spiritual thoughts; and our Lord in the New Testament taught by parables taken from ordinary functions and offices among men that in every trade and calling we might be employed in our worldly business with a heavenly mind—that whether in the shop, or at the loom, or in the field, we might still think of Christ and heaven. There is a parable of merchantmen, a parable of the sower, and a parable of a man calling his servants to an account. In all these parables Christ teaches us that we should be continually thinking of God and heaven. So small a matter as a grain of mustard seed may yield many spiritual applications.

Secondly, there is set and solemn meditation. Now this is of several sorts, or rather they are but several parts of the same exercise. (1.) There is a reflexive meditation, by which we wholly fall upon ourselves. This is nothing else but a solemn conversation between a person and his own heart: "Commune with your own hearts upon your bed, and be still." When in a solemn time alone, reason and inward discourse returns and falls back upon itself. Of all the parts of meditation this is the most difficult, for here a person is to exercise dominion over his soul and to be his own accuser and judge; it is against self-love and carnal ease. We see that all our shifts are to avoid our own company and to run away from ourselves. Guilty man, like a basilisk, dies by seeing himself. Hence the worldly man chokes his soul with business, lest his thoughts, for want of work, like a mill should grind upon itself. The voluptuous person melts away his days in pleasure and charms his soul into a deep sleep with the portion of outward delights, lest it should awake and talk with him. Oh, how necessary it is that a Christian should take some time to consider his ways, to ask of his own soul: "What are we? What have we been? What have we done? What temptations have we passed through, and how have we overcome them?" You would think it strange of two people who conversed every day for forty or fifty years, but all this while did not know one another; yet this is the case between us and our souls; we live a long time in this world but are strangers to ourselves.

(2.) There is a meditation which is more direct and that is of two sorts:

(i.) Instructional, whose object is the Word.
(ii.) Practical, whose object is our lives.

There is more of search and apprehension in the first and more of plot and contrivance in the second. The one is more conversant about doctrines, the other about things. The latter catches hold of the heel of the former, and where instructional meditation ends, there practical meditation begins. (i.) Instructional meditation is when we exercise ourselves in the doctrines of the Word and consider how truths known may be useful to us. It differs from study, partly in the object; study is conversant about a thing unknown in whole or in part: "that you may prove what is the good and acceptable and perfect will of God." However, meditation is an act of knowledge reiterated, or a return of the mind to that point to which it arrived before; it is the inculcation or whetting of a known truth, the pause of reason on something already conceived and known, or a calling to remember what we knew before.

The goal of study is information, but the goal of meditation is practice, or a work upon affections: "This book of the law shall not depart out of your mouth, but you shall meditate therein day and night, that you may observe to do according to all that is written therein."

Study is like a winter's sun that shines but does not heat; but meditation is like the blowing of the fire where we do not mind the blaze but the heat. The fruit of study is to hoard up truth, but the fruit of meditation is to practice it. Curious inquiries have more of the student in them than the Christian. In study we are rather like vintners, who take in wines to store themselves for sale. In meditation we are like customers who buy wine for our use and comfort. A vintner's cellar may be better stored than a customer's, but he has it for others' use. The student may have more of notion and knowledge, his cellar may be better stocked, but he does not have it for taste and necessary refreshment as the Christian does.

(ii.) More practical and application-oriented meditation is when we take ourselves aside from worldly distractions so that we may solemnly consider and study how to carry on the holy life with better success and advantage. "The children of this world are in their generation wiser than the children of light." Here the phrase "in their generation" is a Hebrew phrase for the manner, course, and sphere of our lives: "There are the generations of Noah; Noah was a just man and perfect in his generation, and Noah walked with God." So to be wise in our generation is to be wise in our manner of living and business. So it is said, "He will guide his affairs with discretion," which notes intention and wise foresight, choosing our way, or devising our way. As Solomon states it: "A person's heart devises his way." It is a great part of a Christian's life.

The Scriptures call for this for a minister: "Study to show yourself approved unto God, a workman who does not need to be ashamed, rightly dividing the word of truth," to devise how to carry on his ministry with honor and success. So for private Christians as well: "Let us consider one another, to provoke unto love and to good works." We should consider one another, each other's gifts, dispositions, and graces, so that our spiritual conversation and interaction might be the more improved. By this kind of meditation piety is made more prudent, reasonable, and orderly. Christians who live haphazardly and who order their lives too adventurously, without these rational and wise conversations, are about half as useful as others are. Certainly we should learn this from the children of this world. A wicked person is plotting for his lusts: "Make no provision for the flesh to fulfill the lust thereof." They make provision, and they are catering how they may feed such a lust and satisfy such a carnal desire. Therefore certainly we should take care for the convenience of the holy life, how we may be most useful for God, and pass through our relations with most advantage, and cast our businesses that they may be the least disadvantage to religion, and consider how particular duties may be the most dexterously accomplished: "What shall I render unto the Lord for all his benefits towards me?"

These are the kinds of meditation. The definition may be formed thus: Meditation is that duty or exercise of religion whereby the mind is applied to the serious and solemn contemplation of spiritual things for practical uses and purposes. I shall open the description by the parts of it. 1. It is a duty and exercise of religion. Firstly, that it is a duty and exercise of religion appeared by evidence of Scripture, where it is commanded: "This book of the law shall not depart out of your mouth, but you shall meditate therein day and night." It is made a character of a godly person: "His delight is in the law of the Lord, and in his law he meditates day and night." It is commended in the practice and example of the saints who were most famous in Scripture: Isaac in the present text, Moses and David elsewhere. And as it is plain by the evidence of Scripture, so it is by the light of nature and reason. God who is a Spirit deserves the most pure and spiritual worship, as well as such as is performed by the body. The thoughts are the eldest and noblest offspring of the soul, and the solemn consecration of them is fit for God. Meditation is also called for in the New Testament. I find in the Old Testament the main thing there called for is meditation in the law. In the New Testament we are directed to a new object, the love of Christ: "that you, being rooted and grounded in love, may be able to comprehend with all the saints the breadth, and length, and depth, and height, and to know the love of Christ, which passes knowledge." Meditation suits every way with the nature of our worship: "God is a Spirit, and those who worship him must worship him in spirit and in truth." Now worship in spirit and in truth is agreeable to our state. Meditation is a pure and rational conversation with God: It is the flower and height of consecrated reason.

Secondly, it is not a duty of an arbitrary concern. It is not only a moral help that may be observed or omitted, but a necessary duty without which all graces would languish and wither. Faith is lean and ready to starve unless it is fed with continual meditation on God's promises. As David says: "Unless your law had been my delight, I should have perished in my affliction." Thoughts are the caterers of the soul, which provide for faith and fetch in food and refresh it with the comfort of God's promises. Hope is low and does not arise to such a fullness of expectation till by meditation we take a deliberate view of our hopes and privileges: "Arise, walk through the land, in the length of it, and in the breadth of it, for I will give it unto you."

Our hopes arise according to the largeness of our thoughts. It is a great advantage to have our eyes open to view the riches of inheritance and to have a distinct view of the hope of our calling. The apostle prays for the Ephesians, "that the eyes of your understanding may be enlightened, that you may know what is the hope of his calling, and what the riches of the glory of his inheritance in the saints." People of barren thoughts are usually of low hopes, and for want of getting to the top of Mount Pisgah to view the land, our hearts sink within us. Certainly hope thrives best on the mountain of meditation. Then for love, the sparkles of affection will not flow out unless we beat upon the will of constant thoughts. Affection is nourished by apprehension; and the more constant and deliberate the thoughts are, the deeper the love is.

Those Christians who are backward to the duty of meditation find none of those impulses and melting of love that are in others. They do not endeavor to comprehend the height and breadth and length and depth of the love of Christ, and therefore it is no wonder that their hearts are so narrow and so much straitened towards God. Affections always follow the rate of our thoughts, if they are ponderous and serious. Then comes obedience, or keeping the spirits constantly in a religious frame; to others good motions come like flashes of lightning and are as soon gone as their thoughts are slight and vanishing. But deep musing makes the fire burn and keeps a constant heat and flame in the spirits, not by flashes. And as for duty, so for comfort: A person who is a stranger to meditation is a stranger to himself. In acts of review you enjoy yourselves, and you enjoy yourselves with far more comfort in these private recesses; you most experience God and most experience yourselves. Moses, when he went aside to meditate, had the vision of the fiery bush. Usually God comes in the time of deep meditation, and an elevated heavenly mind is most fit to entertain the comforts and glory of his presence. Thus you see it is a necessary duty. Many think it is an excuse to say it does not suit their temper, that it is a good help only for those who can use it.

I answer. (1.) It is true that there is a great deal of difference among Christians. Some are more serious and consistent and have a greater command of their thoughts; others are of a weaker spirit and are less apt for duties of devotion and contemplation. But our unfitness is usually moral rather than natural, not so much by temper as by disuse; and moral unfitness cannot exempt us from a moral duty. Dirty water cannot wash the hand clean; neither can sin exempt me from a duty. Indisposition, which is a sin in me, does not annul my intimacy with God—as a servant's drunkenness does not excuse him from work. That this is a moral unfitness appears by two things . . .

First, disuse and neglect is the cause of it. Those who use it have a greater command over their thoughts. Men count it a great yoke, but custom would make it easy. Every duty is an aid to itself, and the more we meditate the more we shall be aided. It is pleasant to them who use it: "His delight is in the law of the Lord, and in his law he meditates day and night." Fierce creatures are tame to those who command them, and if a person governed his thoughts, he would find them more obedient.

Second, lack of love. Thoughts are at the service of love; we pause and stay upon such objects as we delight in. Love nails and fastens the soul to the object or thing beloved; as we see we can dwell upon carnal pleasures because our heart is there. Solomon gives this reason why a carnal person cannot dwell upon a solemn object, because "his heart is in the house of amusement." We usually complain that we lack the temper; but the truth is that we lack the heart. David says, "O, how I love your law; it is my meditation all day." Delightful objects will absorb the thoughts.

(2.) Suppose it to be a natural unfitness, yet while you have reason it is not total and universal, and therefore cannot excuse it. We see in other duties that some have the gift of speech and have a great desire for and readiness of expression for prayer; others are more quiet and restrained, but this can be no plea for them wholly to neglect prayer. Duty must be done as we are able; God will hear the breathing, panting soul as well as the rolling tongue. So it is in meditation; some are more talkative and can better melt out their souls in devout communion with God, others can show their love better in zealous actions and public engagements for the glory of Christ. Whatever the case, though there is a diversity of gifts, we are all bound to the same duties, and though we are fitter for some rather than others, yet none may be neglectful.

(3.) The rank and place that meditation has among the duties. Meditation is a middle sort of duty between the Word and prayer and has respect to both. The Word feeds meditation, and meditation feeds prayer; we must hear so that we are not in error, and we must meditate so that we are not barren. These duties must always go hand in hand; meditation must follow hearing but precede prayer.

First, to hear and not to meditate is unfruitful. We may hear and hear, but it is like putting a thing into a bag with holes: "The one who earns wages, earns wages to put it into a bag with holes." "The person is like a man beholding his natural face in a glass; for he beholds himself, and goes his way, and immediately forgets what manner of man he was." Bare hearing begets but transient thoughts, and they leave but a weak impression, which is rather like the glance of a sunbeam upon a wall. There is a glaring for the present, but a person never discerns the beauty, the luster, and the order of the truths delivered till he comes to meditate upon them. Only then can we come clearly to see into the truth, and how it concerns us, and how it falls upon our hearts. David says, "I have more understanding than all my teachers, for your testimonies are my meditation." The preacher can but deliver general theorems and draw them down to practical inferences; by meditation we come to see more clearly and practically than he who preaches. We see, in outward learning, that those who meditate most thrive best. Knowledge floats, till by deliberate thoughts it is compressed upon the affections.

Second, it is dangerous to meditate and not to hear because of errors. A person will soon impose an error upon himself by his own thoughts. Fanatic spirits who neglect listening to the Scriptures pretend to have dreams and revelations. We have a hairsplitter and a heretic in all our hearts, "which soon deceives without a stock and treasure of some knowledge." For people would be vain in their imaginations were not their thoughts corrected by an external light and instruction. Jude called those fanatic persons "filthy dreamers." All practical errors are people's natural imaginations gotten up into a valuable opinion.

Third, it is rashness to pray and not to meditate. What we take in by the Word we digest by meditation and let out by prayer. These three duties must be so ordered that one may not jostle out the other. People are barren, dry, and sapless in their prayers for lack of exercising themselves in holy thoughts: "My heart is indicting a good matter; and then it follows, 'I will speak of the things which I have made touching the King; my tongue is the pen of a ready writer.'" The heart yields matter to the tongue. For meat-offerings in the Old Testament, the oil and the flour were to be kneaded together, and then fried in a pan, and then offered to the Lord. This implies that we must not come with raw dough-baked offerings till we have concocted and prepared them by mature deliberation. It is notable that often in Scripture prayer is called by the name of meditation because it is the product and issue of it: "Give ear to my words, O Lord; consider my meditation." This implies that the psalmist's prayer was but the expression of his deliberate and premeditated thoughts. So elsewhere: "Let the words of my mouth and the meditation of my heart be acceptable in your sight, O Lord, my strength and my redeemer." Meditation is the vent of the thoughts.

2. Whereby the mind is applied to the serious and solemn consideration. I add this to distinguish it from occasional meditation and those good thoughts that accidentally rush into our minds and to note the care and intenseness of the soul in such an exercise: Through desire a person, having separated himself, seeks and intermeddles with all wisdom. Then a person is fit for these solemn and holy thoughts and for intermeddling with all wise and divine matters—namely, when he has divorced himself from other cares and is able to keep his knowledge under a wise confinement.

3. Of spiritual things. This is, for instance, God, that we may fear him; sin, that we may abhor it; the works of God, that we may glorify the Creator. They refer to any useful object. So David limits it: "My mouth shall speak of wisdom; and the meditation of my heart shall be of understanding." He means the state and end of man. Generally the object in the Old Testament is the law.

4. For practical uses and inferences. This notes the end. Meditation is not to puzzle the head with notions, but to better the heart. The proper use of this exercise is to set on those great practical heads of religion, to work the heart to a greater care of duty and hatred of sin. To a greater care of duty: "I will meditate in your precepts, and have respect for your ways," and to a greater hatred of sin: "I have hid your word in my heart that I might not sin against you."

8

Manton as Public Figure: Living as a Christian Citizen

[T]he commonwealth must be made to agree with the church. . . . As it is the foundation of the world, it is appropriate that the commonwealth, which is built upon that foundation, should be framed according to the church.

Thomas Cartwright

In an age like this, [Thomas] Manton occupied for several years a very prominent position. He was not a country parson, living scores of miles from London, and absorbed in unobtrusive pastoral labors among a rural population. On the contrary, he was a standard-bearer in the fore-front of the battle . . . a man who could neither say, nor do, nor write anything without being observed.

J. C. Ryle

Dr. Manton was not so unknown to London, nor is he so much forgotten, as that his name or writings should need any of my commendations. . . . [He was so] sound in judgment against extremes in the controversies of these times.

Richard Baxter

Introduction

It is a commonly known fact that the English Reformation was different from the Protestant Reformations on the Continent. Although figures such as Martin Luther and Ulrich Zwingli were rightly known as "magisterial reformers" because they were aligned with the magistrates or civil authorities, the English Reformation was even more entangled with the state. Beginning with Henry VIII's marital problems with his wife Catherine of Aragon, the reformation in England began with an act of state and continued to be wholly influenced by state politics well into Thomas Manton's time.

In fact, an act of state is exactly what ensued as a result of the king's great matter. The Act of Supremacy, which the English Parliament passed in November of 1534, was the beginning of the English Reformation. This act of state granted King Henry VIII complete sovereignty over the Church in England. It declared that Henry was "the only supreme head on earth of the Church of England," thereby repudiating the previous authority of the pope. The king immediately began reaping the benefits of his new office as he dissolved hundreds of monasteries and redirected revenue toward the crown rather than Rome. The English monarchy would continue to directly influence the state of the church for 100 years, until Charles I was executed by Parliament in 1649 and Oliver Cromwell took control of the government for about a decade. When Charles II, the son of Charles I, was (re-)instated as king at the Restoration in 1660, politics continued to interrelate with the church.

Manton's Preaching before Parliament

All of these events set the scene for Thomas Manton's role as a citizen in England. Manton, to state the obvious, was just as involved in state affairs as he was in religious ones. Not only did Manton preach at the inauguration of Oliver Cromwell to the Protectorship, he also served as a chaplain to Richard Cromwell, Oliver's son who reigned after him for less than a year, as well as to Charles II when his line was restored. In addition to his role as chaplain to

8.1. Portrait of Oliver Cromwell, who ruled England during the 1650s.

three different English monarchs and leaders, Manton was called on several occasions to preach before Parliament. Beginning in 1647, he would be called to preach before this great assembly six or seven times.

To preach before Parliament was an honorable yet precarious invitation to accept, for the nation was in the middle of a civil war, and people on all sides—clergymen not excluded—were expendable. Just two years before Manton began preaching before Parliament, for instance, Archbishop William Laud was beheaded, and more than a year before Manton preached at the installation of Oliver Cromwell as Lord Protector, Manton's good friend and pastoral colleague Christopher Love likewise lost his head for treason and crimes against the state.

In the sermon that follows, Manton boldly addresses many of the different issues that the nation was facing.[1] The date of the sermon is June 30, 1647. Manton is preaching before the Long Parliament, and the country is in the middle of the English Civil War. But instead of arguing that the state has no role in the affairs of the church as some Puritans would do, Manton argues the opposite. The state was to be instrumental in producing a holy commonwealth. Although God was in the process of punishing the nation as a whole for its collective sin against God, the Lord was not finished with this English nation. What was needed was repentance at the state level, since the state was believed to be ordained by God to make the mission and morals of Christianity prevail.

A Sermon Preached before the Parliament by Thomas Manton

"It shall come to pass in that day that there will be no light; the lights will diminish. It will be one day which is known

---

1. *The Complete Works of Thomas Manton* (Worthington, PA: Maranatha Publications, 1900), 15:179–87.

to the LORD—neither day nor night. But at evening time it shall happen that it will be light" (Zech. 14:6–7).

These words are a notable prophecy, and, as all prophecies are, they are somewhat obscure. Your attempts to get to the bottom of them will not be successful. At this time I will not dispute the meaning and particular application of the events described—that is, whether they relate to the general state of the times between Christ's ascension and his second coming or to some special season when this passage will be most eminently fulfilled. Rather, let it suffice to note that there is here, first, a description of troublesome times and, second, a prescription of comforts against the troubles of them.

I. The description of troublesome times: And it shall come to pass in that day that the light will be neither clear nor dark.
II. A prescription of comforts, with three observances:
1. The brief occurrence of them: It shall be one day, that is, one period of providence.
2. The providential ordination and disposal of them: known to the Lord.
3. The end and issue of them: At evening it shall be light. There are two things expressed: The event will provide comfort, and it will be at an unusual time: at evening.

To explain these parts. First, the state of the times. By light and darkness and day and night is meant prosperity and adversity, truth and falsehood, joy and sorrow, hopes and fears. Now, when it is said that it will be neither light nor dark, the meaning is neither good nor bad to either extreme: neither applause nor complaint, neither completely day nor completely night—instead, a mixture of both.

Second, the comforts produced. 1. It will be one day: one period or course of providence. God's people may meet with sharp encounters here in the world and be kept in much uncertainty as to their outward comforts; but the time is short. It is short in itself, short in comparison of eternity, short in regard to their own desolation, short with respect to the enemies' rage, short with respect to our love to God.

2. Known to the Lord: that is, determined or appointed by him. Nothing happens to us without God's providence and special designation. He has set the time, and also lessens every ounce of that bitter cup we drink of with his own hand.

3. The issue and end: Towards morning it will be light. It will end well, and that at such a time when nobody would look for it. All provision to God's church ends in light, and this at the evening, when sun and day is gone, when seemingly all things tend to a new calamity and are ready to introduce a sad night and extreme darkness. When miseries first seize upon us we are full of hopes; and when things begin to clear up and look hopeful, we say, "Now it will end," and "Then it will end," even though it may be but the beginning of the day or morning of our troubles. But at evening, when our hopes are quite spent and we give all for lost, then unexpected deliverance breaks in, and we come to the end of all our troubles.

First, observe that the day of the church's conflict is intermixed and displays God's unpredictable providences. Sometimes truth and righteousness get the upper hand; and sometimes those things that produce error and unrighteousness do. Now, it is a doubtful day in a twofold regard: (i) because light and darkness are either intermixed or alternate (a) either because they shine together at the same time or they succeed each other in turns, or (b) because crosses and comforts, troubles or successes are equally poised, and a man cannot say which is greater, the light or darkness. (ii) Or else because our estate in respect of either is not durable and fixed, but liable to great uncertainties. We do not know which will prevail in the end. Let me illustrate the point in either sense.

1. There are two conflicting kinds of providence at the same time, and the church is in several respects both happy and miserable at once. Here things go well, there poorly. Things may be difficult in private when it may be well in public—as Paul rejoiced when the gospel was freely preached, though from prison. Or it may be well with us when it is not well with the church. It is a rare case when there is a perfect harmony between our private condition and public happiness. Jacob was at once afraid when hearing of Esau's four hundred men, but was relieved at the sight of a host of angels sent to guard him. The angel that wrestled with him blessed him, but also handicapped him. Paul had wonderful revelations, but also a thorn in his flesh. These are strange ways to illustrate providence: Good and evil are interwoven with one another in a strange way. There is some evil to show we are not past all danger, but there is some good to show we are not shut out from all hope. God is like a wise pilot who takes in as much weight as the ship will allow but without sinking it.

2. There is simultaneously an up and down of conditions: Good and evil succeed each other in turns. This can be seen in the state of the Jewish church. Saul's time was bad, David's and Solomon's good, Rehoboam's and Abijah's bad, Asa's and Jehoshaphat's good, and so on. This is how God works with his people in the world. Take, for instance, the time of Hezekiah. After coming to the crown, he prospered for many years; but the tide soon turned. Sennacherib invaded his country and seized everything. But when he prayed, God

delivered him by a miracle, destroying Sennacherib's host. Then Hezekiah gets sick and is ready to die; but instead of dying, fifteen years are added to his life. After this, his heart was lifted up. But finally wrath came upon him—a sad message concerning the calamities of his posterity. What a strange series of events! Up and down, day and night, light and dark. The church is in danger of being ruined. Human affairs, under God, depend much on the people's hearts, and how uncertain are they! Those who cry "Hosanna" today tomorrow cry "Crucify." Peter makes a glorious confession, and a little afterward a sickening denial. Paul was received as an angel of God, and then looked upon as an enemy.

Second, The reason of this, why the day of our conflict is each a mixed doubtful day. Let us consider: (1) The equity and (2) the wisdom of God in it.

1. The equity of it. It is such a day as is very suitable to our condition in the world. Firstly, we are in a middle place, between heaven and hell, and therefore partake somewhat of both. Hell is set forth by utter darkness, and of heaven it is said, "There is no night there." It is all day or all night in the other world; but here neither day nor night, neither clear nor dark. It is convenient that this middle place of trial should have somewhat of both. In hell there is all evil and only evil, without any temperament of mercy; and in heaven, no more death, nor sorrow, nor crying, nor any pain anymore. These pleased spirits are ever rejoicing. God would give a taste of the other world in the present life: of eternal death and eternal life in the sorrows and comforts of the present life. It will not be too well nor too ill in the world.

Secondly, we have mixed principles: flesh and spirit. And as long as sin remains in us we cannot be perfectly happy. The flesh needs to be weakened by diverse afflictions: as grace to be encouraged, and love cherished, with experiences and proofs of God's favor; clouds and sunshine, frowns and favors, summer and winter, day and night. I speak of the best. Alas, generally we are "evil, only evil, and that continually," and therefore our condition might be so.

Thirdly, as our principles are mixed, so are all our operations. There is a mixture of good and evil in all our services. The water receives a tincture from the channel through which it passes. Our duties are spotted and stained; there is iniquity in holy things; indeed, our zealous undertakings and engagements for Christ have a tang of the flesh. There is a great deal of wrath, revenge, fleshly zeal, and kitchen-fire, rather than a coal of the altar, while we are engaged for God. "Our righteousness is as filthy rags; we are as a dried leaf; our iniquities have taken us away." None of our actions are free from default and defilement.

2. The wisdom and justice of God in it. He has many wise ends to be accomplished by these mixed providences. Firstly, God gives us mixed providences so that a people worn out with long misery may be more pliable to God's purpose. By such mixed providences God will weaken and waste stubborn natures and cause them to be tossed up and down, that by the protraction of their miseries he may work them to his own bent. A cloud that is soon blown over and only gets us wet a little in the passing is not regarded; but when the conflict is long between light and darkness, sunshine and storms, and our miseries continue longer, it awakens a people to inquire after God's mind. For a great while a people make a light matter of religion, and God's interest in the nation is looked upon as a trifle, not worth the looking after, and therefore there is such slight reformation; but before God is done with them they will see that his interests are to be regarded as well as other rights of man. Surely God has some notable work to do upon England, or else he would not pursue us with so many effects of his anger and break

us with so many changes and distractions. Are all these shakings to no purpose? Are they to leave us there where God found us in the beginning? As unholy and unreformed as before? Surely, then, it will be utter ruin: "Because I would have purged you, and you were not purged, you should not be purged from your filthiness anymore." But God seems not to leave England so much so that he would say, "Let them alone:" As it is with a natural body, when corruption has seized upon the vital parts and the body must be brought very low and just kept alive, that a better spring of blood may be procured, the wise physician gives nothing for a while that may strengthen nature, lest it strengthen the disease; so when corruptions are so chronic, rooted in people's minds, God wears us out with a continual vicissitude and interchange of providences. His dispensations are somewhat like those supplies the Athenians gave to a lingering war, just enough to keep it up, not to end it. Demosthenes compares them to a medicinal diet, which neither strengthens nor suffers to die, till it grows to a lingering mischief. As by the motions of his Spirit, so by the courses of his providence: "God speaks once, and twice, and man does not perceive it." God is loath to be gone and make it whole night, and loath to tarry and make it perfect day, but sometimes one party prevails, sometimes another. Oh, that we were wise!

Secondly, God gives us mixed providences in order to work us from earthly to heavenly things. In heaven there is no night but all day. There is no stability in outward comforts, that we may look higher and get "the moon under our feet." All sublunary things are liable to changes. We are eagerly bent upon temporal happiness and would seek our rest here, but God makes all unquiet to drive us higher. Noah's ark, when it was tossed upon the waves, was the nearer to heaven; so the more we are tossed upon the unstable waters, the more should we look after the place of our eternal rest, where we will be forever with the Lord.

Thirdly, God gives us mixed providences to put a cloud and veil upon his actions. There is a foolish curiosity that possesses us; we are usually earnest to know the event, but slack to use the means; it is natural for us to inquire after what is to come, and to neglect present duties. Now no creature will know the bottom of God's counsels. When he means to be a savior, the world will not know so much, but things are kept in a doubtful uncertainty, and we cannot say whether they tend to ruin or establishment: "In the days of prosperity be joyful, and in the day of adversity consider: God has set the one against the other, to the end that man may find nothing after him." This is so that man is not able to look to the end of God's design, since man makes decisions not upon reasons of conscience but with carnal motives; and therefore when man is upon his trial, the face of things look doubtful.

Fourthly, God gives us mixed providences to prevent the excesses of either condition. God tempers and qualifies the one with the other. Prosperity makes us grow wanton; adversity makes us grow stupid. Therefore, that we may mourn as if we mourned not, and rejoice as if we rejoiced not, we are exercised with various changes. Out of indulgence to us God gives us prosperity, lest we should be overwhelmed with sorrow; and then he gives us adversity again for the abuse of prosperity. The one is set against the other, to keep the soul in an equal temper and poise. In adversity we think we will never be delivered; in prosperity we think we will never be moved. Now, to keep the soul steady, God seems to hover, and the face of providence looks with a doubtful uncertainty. When stormy winds fill the sails, it is hard to go steady. It is certainly a help to harden our thoughts to changes; but when we are well at ease we are apt to forget. Few say, as David, "Surely man at his best estate is altogether vanity." We should rejoice with trembling. Leaven (which was forbidden in other Jewish sacrifices) was allowed in thank-offerings. Leaven made bread sour to taste. When we offer praise for any benefits and deliverances, we should still entertain suitable thoughts of our bitterness in the present state. God gives us such mixed providences that we may neither surfeit in prosperity nor despond in adversity, neither wax wanton nor be swallowed up of sorrow.

Fifthly, God gives us mixed providences to make way for the exercise of our faith. Therefore, in the tenor of his providence, God so governs and orders his providential dispensations towards his people that they will not live by sense but by faith. To make this evident, let me tell you five possible ways that providence may be imagined.

i. The first is that the righteous will always see good, and the wicked suffer evil.

ii. The second is that the righteous will always be afflicted and meet with nothing but evil in the world, and the wicked be always prosperous and enjoy good.

iii. The third is that both good and evil people should always be afflicted and never see a good day in the world.

iv. The fourth is that both good and bad people should be always prosperous and never troubled with any evil.

v. The fifth is that there should be neither evil, and only evil, for the wicked, nor good, and only good, for the righteous, but a mixture of both: to the good, sometimes good; and to the evil, sometimes evil.

Now, though all these ways of providence might be just, yet God does only the first and the last of these: the first in the world to come, the last in the present life, that is to say, that the righteous should enjoy good, and only good, and the wicked evil and only evil. This is the dispensation that God reserves for the world to come, where the good are always and completely blessed, and the wicked are always and completely miserable. God has chosen the last for this world: a mixture of good and evil promiscuously dispensed; that is to say, that some good people enjoy more of worldly prosperity, others are kept low and bare; and that there should be vicissitudes in the same person: some comforts, some crosses. On the other side, the wicked should be sometimes mighty and prosperous, and sometimes that the iniquity of their heels should cleave to them. There are intermixtures, that neither the righteous nor the wicked may be known by their outward condition.

Why? Because the present state is a state of faith, not a state of sense. We are justified by faith, we live by faith, we walk by faith, and not by sight; therefore this state of faith requires that the manner by which God governs the world should neither be too sensible and clear nor too obscure and dark, but a middle thing—as the daybreak or twilight is between the light of the day and the full darkness of the night. If too clear, we would not need faith. If too obscure, we would wholly lose faith.

Therefore, the first way of providence is not fit for the present world, that the godly will always be happy and flourish and have all things according to their heart's desire, and the wicked always in troubles and calamities. This would make religion too sensible a thing, unfit for the present time, when we walk by faith and not by sense. If the world were so governed, it could not be put to any trial; and temporal things, the good and evil of the present time, would be the great motives to induce men to serve God and avoid sin. Therefore, that men may live by faith and look for a better reward of righteousness and a greater punishment of sin, God will not always observe this law and course in his dispensations, to bestow upon the good the blessings of the world and inflict upon the evil the punishments thereof but promiscuously give good things to the wicked, that they may not be thought the chiefest good, and sometimes he will bestow them upon the good, that the very possession of these may not be thought evil. Sometimes he will be glorified by his servants in a high and prosperous condition, and sometimes in a low and afflicted one. And they will enjoy vicissitudes and interchanges; sometimes no complaining in their families, sometimes great breaches made upon them. Therefore the first way may be fit for heaven, but it is not fit for earth. It would make all things liable to sense if God had distinguished men by their outward condition. No, in these things he deals promiscuously: "All things come alike to all." He does not promiscuously dispense the riches of his grace; these are invisible treasures. His Christ, his Spirit, the hopes of glory he gives only to the good; but health, wealth, beauty, strength, success, children are promiscuously given to good and bad; and God will take them, as well as give them, at his pleasure.

But now all the other ways of providence, as the second, third, fourth, would too much obscure the providence of God and hinder faith; as the second, that the righteous should always see evil, and the wicked enjoy the good things of this world. Alas, if we were held always in misery and affliction, and the wicked should always wallow in pomp and ease and plenty, it would be a grievous temptation to the weak to deny providence. Indeed, the faith of the strongest would be grievously shaken, for we cannot expect that the good should be perfect in an instant and presently dead to all temporal interests. If now, when we see some good people oppressed while the evil rejoice, we are so apt to question, as the Israelites did—"Is the Lord amongst us, yes or no?"— what would be done then? And who could keep his patience and keep his faith if the wicked were always kept in joy and triumph while the godly are in tears? Therefore God mixes his dispensations. Sometimes, to exercise our faith and patience, he denies many things to his friends that he bestows upon his enemies; yet often, on the other side, God punishes the wicked and rewards the godly, to show his providence. And so faith is neither made void by too great a light, nor extinguished by too great a darkness.

Concerning the third sort of providence, that both should be always miserable, both wicked and godly: if both were alike afflicted there would be no knowledge of the goodness of God till the world to come, no invitations to repentance nor sense of the mercy of the creation to invite us to remember God. All our pleasant affections would be useless, and our graces, which serve for delighting in God, would be cut off and prevented. The harmony and order of the world disturbed, which has cast the world into hills and valleys, appoints some to be in prosperity, others in affliction and want, that the happy may have occasions of showing mercy and relieving the miserable—as the great veins in the body abound with blood to fill the lesser. But chiefly God would not then show his bounty to all his creatures as he does: "He makes his sun to arise upon the evil and the good, and sends rain upon the just and unjust." "He did not leave himself without witness in that he was good and gave us rain from heaven and fruitful seasons."

This world is a common inn, where God entertains sons and bastards and seeks to draw and allure them to repentance by his goodness. He would have the wicked wonder why they have all this wealth, honor and greatness, houses and fields, servants and provisions. *Did I bring them into the world with me when I was born, or did a good God provide them for me? No, I came into the world naked. Did I acquire them by my own wit and industry? No, many who are better than me in these things lack them. Did I gain them by inheritance? Who made me to be born of rich parents, not of poor ones? Many more righteous than I are in a difficult estate of life; surely it was God who prevented these things from happening to me with his goodness and mercy, and shall I be unthankful for these benefits?* God would stir up these thoughts in the minds of men.

We should not look to the fourth sort of providence, that both the good and the evil should be continually happy. For then there would be no room for suffering graces, for the exercise of fortitude and patience, contempt of the world and self-denial. The best would soon forget the world to come. David would not have the Canaanites utterly destroyed to keep Israel in exercise: "Do not slay them, lest my people forget." When there was great deliberation in the senate of Rome whether Carthage should be utterly destroyed, Scipio was against it, that the Roman youth might be kept in exercise by an envious city. And the event showed the soundness of his advice, for the ruin of Carthage was the ruin of Rome, for being corrupted by prosperity, they fell into all licentiousness, and for want of a potent adversary to keep them in breath and exercise, they fell into destructive divisions and seditions among themselves. It is said, "The prosperity of fools destroys them." Well, then, you see the reasons for this mixed dispensation.

But is not this contrary to that faith and dependence that we should have upon God for present mercies, when there is such a doubtful face of things that men do not know what certainly to expect, since certainty is the ground of faith and close trust?

I answer that "godliness has the promises of this life, and that which is to come," and that God does not truly cast off his people and leave them to shift for themselves in temporal things: "For the Lord will not cast off his people, nor forsake his inheritance." Men may cast them off, and God may hide himself from them for a while, but yet he takes care of them.

He may for a time correct and chastise them and permit them for a while to abide under sharp oppressions; yet he will not utterly forsake them but will support and deliver them in his own season. But the faith that is required of us is not a certain expectation of temporal events; there God leaves it to a maybe. If outward things were sure, we should live by sense rather than faith. God will be waited upon and therefore keeps the disposal of all things in his own hand— God keeps it as doubtful. The true generous faith is not a confidence of particular success, but a committing of ourselves to God's power and referring ourselves to his will; as the leper says, "Lord, if you will, you can make me clean."

Sixthly, God gives us mixed providences to win the heart by the various methods of judgments and mercies, and to gain upon us by both means at once: "I will sing of judgment and mercy; unto you, O Lord, I will sing." It may be neither day nor night, but both together, that our fears and hopes may draw us to God. Mixed graces do best. To increase our fear, God lets out trouble; to encourage us to hope in God, that trouble is checked by other providences. The wind blows, but God keeps it from growing furious. "Though I walk in the midst of trouble, you will revive me."

Seventhly, God gives us mixed providences to bring his people to a Christian union and accord. God will not hear one sort of his people against another. When religion's interest is divided, God keeps the balance equal, and success is sometimes cast on this side, sometimes on that one. The light shines sometimes in one hemisphere, sometimes in another; every side comes on the stage, has their success, and manifests their corruptions and cannot bear one with another. God breaks this confidence and that one, then draws to a union. This is so that at length we may lay down our enmities and oppositions and "not bite and devour one another, lest at length we be consumed one of another."

Sometimes the strength and upper hand is given to these; they carry the day, but not the complete victory. What does this suggest but that we should end the difference by compromise and reconciliation, lest, while we weaken one another by our mutual differences, the whole church be made a prey to Satan and his emissaries, and inevitable ruin and destruction light upon the whole. What have we gained by our contests? Stumbling-blocks are multiplied, atheists are increased. Oh, when shall that spirit prevail, "There is a tribe lacking in Israel"? Though they fought against them, yet they owned them as brothers. Alas, one faction is getting the ball from another, and our church divisions are but like a game of football. Surely, though two seeds will not be reconciled, yet God's family may be reconciled. Now where principles are such as may let in somewhat of Christ, we should try all means; we cannot wholly separate till our master be gone before us. If they fly from peace, we must pursue it.

Eighthly, God gives us mixed providences to prevent contempt and ruin towards those who have fallen under God's displeasure. This is to "persecute them whom God has destroyed, and to speak to the grief of those whom God has wounded." "Do not rejoice when your enemy falls, and do not let your heart be glad when he stumbles, lest the Lord see it, and it displease him, and he turn away his wrath from him." A vindictive spirit is a transgression of God's law. To rejoice and insult over misery is the worst sort of revenge.

Ninthly, God gives us mixed providences so it is a ground of patience: "Shall we receive good at the hand of God, and not evil?" Heavy afflictions do not lack their comforts to make them tolerable. We do not want mixtures to support us. He measures out good and evil with a great deal of wisdom and tenderness. Should not they who have received good things from the Lord be content to submit to evil things or afflictions when God sees fit to do so? The tide will ebb and flow.

We would have it always flow; but God will not ask our leave and consent and govern affairs by our opinion, but will send good and evil as it pleases him. Therefore, as we receive and entertain good things thankfully and cheerfully, so it is our duty to receive evil things submissively and contentedly. It is a great fault to limit God to one way of dealing with his people, that we cannot endure changes. We must resolve for good and evil, and prepare for it. Vicissitudes in our condition are necessary for us. A settled ease in the world would soon corrupt us. In short, God freely confers good things upon us; and therefore we should not take it ill if sometimes he makes us taste the bitter fruits of our own deserts. A Christian should be prepared for new assaults of trouble.

Tenthly, God gives us mixed providences to show that our comforts and crosses are in his hand; and he variously dispenses weal or woe as our condition requires: "I form the light, and create darkness; I make peace, and create evil; I the Lord do all these things." When he gives quietness, who then can make trouble? And when he hides his face, who then can behold him? God peppers his providence unpredictably, that if we will not take notice of him in one dispensation, we may in another. "The day is yours, and the night is yours; you have prepared the light and the sun; you have made summer and winter." It is spoken of a deep time of trouble. He who has set winter and summer, day and night, one against another, has also set good and evil in the life of man.

You must not so understand it as if good came from God and evil from ourselves or by chance. No, God's hand is to be seen and owned in both. He is our party; therefore our first business is to reconcile ourselves to God, to please him, to bear the evil patiently, to accept the good thankfully from his hand. None can resist or remedy what God is pleased to do. God has power to help and power to cast down; and in both he works sovereignly and irresistibly. Dangers and deliverances, troubles and consolations come all from him. He will exercise us in various ways: fearing, believing, trembling, rejoicing, mourning, giving thanks.

Application. Now what use should we make of all this? 1. Be sure you do not make an ill use of it. Firstly, when we are not thankful for our mercies because they are not full and perfect. That is a proud and murmuring spirit that entertains crosses with anger and blessings with disdain. What but this is spoken of, "Wherein have you loved us?" As the people murmured in the wilderness when they came out of Egypt, we disvalue what we have in comparison of what we expect. Pliny speaks of some: Forget what is granted, pitch only upon what is denied—as children in a tantrum throw away what they have if you do not give them more: "All this," Haman says, "avails me nothing." As in the body, if one humor is out of order or one joint broken, the soundness of the rest is not regarded, so apt are we to murmur if all is not done at once. Though God may see it needful to keep you in fears and uncertainties, and you do not have all that you look for, yet acknowledge what you do have. Do not say, "It is but so and so, a truce rather than a peace." God is making a step onward in England's mercies. There are many strange providences that bring us to this. It is a mercy that he remembered us in our low estate, when all was struck at; honor and religious worship and property were at stake, and he gave us some breathing and rest after our oppressions, some ease after toil, as plowmen give their oxen after they come from work. And now the union of the Parliament with their brothers is a step further; we hope we are growing towards the glorious evening. It is an ill use not to acknowledge mercies if all things are not according to your minds. Do not say, "It is but thus and thus." "Who has despised the day of small things?" It is God's way to begin with small things that promise only a little; thankfulness is the way to make them greater. God is at work; tarry till he brings it forth to perfection.

Secondly, it is an abuse if we are discouraged in God's service because of this uncertainty and the returning of clouds after rain, so that you cannot tell whether it will be day or night. You ought to take God's part: as in the combat between flesh and spirit, to come into the relief of the better part, so it is in this doubtful conflict. (i) When you have any respite and breathing-time, then is a time and season to put your hand to the work: "I must do the works of him who sent me while it is today; the night comes when none can work." Blessed be God, it is not night with us. Truth is not wholly banished, nor buried under a night of ignorance, error, and superstitions; nor is the comfort of prosperity wholly gone. While it is day, let us do something for God's interest. (2) If there are uncertainties, understand that a great work is never brought to pass without troubles, and duty should be welcome to you even though you are uncertain of the event. Go about it with a resolute submission to God's will and as prepared for all occasions. This is a Christian spirit. When you come upon temporal happiness altogether and a settled estate in the world, you will be deceived. (3) Change does not come till our condition proves a snare to us; till we grow neglectful of God and his interest, as if we could do well without him, and use our power against him, and so provoke him to leave us.

2. The right use we should make of it. When we have mixed dispensations and are under an uncertain conflict, then . . . Firstly, by way of caution, take heed of human confidences and of presuming too much of temporal success. One great reason of this long uncertainty wherein England is exercised is because we run from one means to another and do not take up the controversy between us and God. It may be said to

us, as to Israel, "Why do you run to and fro, one while in this manner, another while in another, to seek establishment here and there, like a sick man turning in his bed?" Then the threatening is, "You shall go forth with your hands upon your head; for the Lord has rejected your confidences, and you shall not prosper in them." Come back with a heavy heart and dejected condition. As clapping the hands is an expression of joy, so going forth with their hands upon their heads is a sign of great sorrow. In the issue it would turn to extreme grief and anguish of heart. It is not improper, now that you are fit to rejoice in God, to remind you of these things. I do not speak this to take you away from the use of means, but from trusting in means: Oh, this will do it, and that will do it. I tell you, it is the Lord who must do it.

But when do we trust in means, you may ask? When we use the creature without God and hope to work out our ends without giving God his ends. When we try to get rid of misery by fleshly aid, human force and counsel, without humiliation and repentance and serious returning to the Lord. When we set the creature against God by wicked combinations and cover it with a covering, that we may add sin to sin. When we carry on an evil purpose, to accept vileness, that a profane spirit may again come upon the stage and sin triumphantly.

If we have this in design, it is to set means against God. Sometimes we set up the creature above God, as if his blessing were nothing to human preparations; and our hearts run more upon outward helps than his favor and blessing. "When Ephraim saw his sickness, and Judah saw his wound, then Ephraim sent to king Jareb, yet he could not heal you, nor cure you of your wound." Sometimes we yoke the creature with God when we confine his providence to our probabilities, as if God could work no other way out that which we fancy: "They turned back, and tempted God, and limited the Holy One of Israel." We do no more than we see reason for in the course of second causes. I tell you, God is the main party; it is with him this nation has to do; it is not with unquiet libertines, with open enemies, but with God.

Finally, for direction . . . First, walk by a sure rule: "Your word is a lamp to my feet, a light to my path." Civil interests are determined by the laws of the country where we live. So far as concerns conscience, the Word of God is a rule and sure direction. When you consult with it—what would God have me do in such a case?—you shall be sure to know his mind and your own duty, and so can suffer and act the more cheerfully.

Second, get a sure guide: "Trust in the Lord with all your heart, and lean not to your own understanding; in all your ways acknowledge him, and he shall direct your paths." We have no more understanding than as God is pleased to confirm to us from day to day. Magistrates are bidden to be instructed: "Be wise now therefore, O you kings; be instructed, you judges of the earth." Their good and evil is of a public influence. When men make their hearts their oracles, their own wits their counselors—especially when swayed by their passions and corrupt affections—they usually miscarry.

Last, encourage yourselves by the sure promises that you have to build upon: "the sure mercies of David." The righteous have a sure reward: "To him who sows righteousness will be a sure reward." Heaven is a kingdom that cannot be shaken: "Therefore, receiving a kingdom that cannot be moved, let us have grace whereby we may serve God acceptably, with reverence and godly fear." There are great alterations here, but in heaven all is stable; there is joy without any mixture of sorrow: no misery, no weakness to perplex. In short, a person wrapped up in the peace of God and the quiet of a good conscience and hopes of eternal life is fortified against all encounters, storms, and difficulties whatsoever.

9

MANTON AS PREACHER: LEARNING ABOUT JESUS AND HIS CALL TO DENIAL

The first and principal duty of a pastor is to feed the flock by
diligent preaching of the Word.
Richard Baxter

As an expositor of Scripture, I regard Manton with
unmingled admiration.
J. C. Ryle

Manton presents us with the best that English Puritans had to
offer in careful, solid, warmhearted exposition of the Scriptures.
Joel Beeke

Introduction

The Reformed tradition is one that systematically preaches
and teaches the Scriptures. Going back to the early sixteenth
century to figures like Ulrich Zwingli and John Calvin, it was
Reformed pastors who first replaced the Catholic liturgy with
biblical preaching. The reason for this focus is evident in the

Second Helvetic Confession (1562), for instance, wherein author Heinrich Bullinger writes that "the preaching of the Word of God is the Word of God." Whereas the Catholic tradition in which Zwingli, Calvin, and Bullinger were raised focused supremely on the Eucharist, which was understood to become and contain Christ's body, those in the Reformed tradition concentrated on the preaching of the gospel in Scripture. Over the course of the next several decades, Reformed teachers in England like William Perkins vigorously continued this practice of "prophecy," which is chiefly defined as "preaching the Word."

As the English and Reformed pastor Thomas Manton approached the weekly task of preaching and teaching the Scriptures, he did so in the knowledge that he was engaged in a significant practice within the church. Rather than just conducting the liturgy in the Book of Common Prayer, he was preaching the Word of God. What he preached, therefore, was of paramount importance. Fellow Puritan preacher Thomas Brooks once wrote that there are three areas of the Christian life that should receive the most attention, all of which are to come from a biblically based knowledge: Christ, Satan's devices, and our own hearts. Manton preached on all of these areas, and it would not be an exaggeration to state that there are elements of all of them in each of his sermons—Christ being paramount. When beginning the

9.1. Medal of Ulrich Zwingli, the first Reformer to preach verse-by-verse on Sundays, rather than following the liturgy.

first of several sermons on Isaiah 53, for instance, Manton quickly points out that "the prophecy of Isaiah" in this chapter should rather be called "the gospel of Isaiah." His other sermons testify to how diligently he preached about Christ.

Manton's Sermon on Self-Denial

In the sermon that follows, Manton refers to all the doctrines that Brooks mentioned above: Christ, Satan's devices, as well as our own hearts.[1] As an excerpt illustrates,

> Your self-denial must be out of . . . love to Christ. And you must not do it casually, but with your whole heart. There is no such great self-seeking as is carried on usually under the color of self-denial, [for] the devil disguises himself into all forms and shapes. . . .

Specifically in this sermon, Manton touches on one of the most central commands of Jesus in the Gospels: denying the pleasures of our own hearts for the sake of Christ. As usual, Manton is not content to preach a sermon and move on. He dwells on the passage, and the following sermon is merely one of eight that he preached on this passage. In the sermon Manton not only offers the reasons and the evidences of self-denial, but he also provides the solutions, namely, becoming more and more like Christ and becoming less and less like ourselves. The date of the sermon series is not known.

A Treatise of Self-Denial

"If anyone will come after me, let him deny himself." (Matt. 16:24)

1. *The Complete Works of Thomas Manton* (Worthington, PA: Maranatha Publications, 1900), 17:263–73.

Introduction. The occasion of these words is as follows: Christ had foretold his passion, and Peter took offense. The cross, though it is the badge of Christianity, is always displeasing to flesh and blood; and we dislike heaven, not for itself, but for the way we travel to the land of promise: through a howling wilderness. Fleshly fancy imagines a path strewed with lilies and roses. We are too tenderfooted to think of briers and thorns.

Peter gives vent to his distaste by carnal counsel: "Master, favor yourself." Peter's speech to his master is much like the voice of the flesh or Satan in our own hearts; when duty cannot be done without difficulty and disadvantages, our carnal hearts say, "Favor yourself, let this be far from you." Christ rebuked Peter, or rather the devil in Peter: "Get behind me, Satan." God's own children may often play Satan's game. Peter speaks out of an innocent affection and respect to his master, and the devil has a hand in it. And therefore it is a high point of spiritual wisdom to be skilled in his enterprises. "We are not ignorant of his devices," says the apostle. The devil turns and twists on every hand; the same Satan who stirred up the high priests to crucify Christ sets his own disciple upon him, to dissuade him from being crucified. Peter was afraid of the work of redemption and therefore sought either to hinder the sufferings of Christ or to make them so shameful that the scandal might take off from the efficacy. When Christ was upon the cross the devil played the same game, but by other instruments: "If you are the Son of God, come down from the cross." Though he had our Savior at that pass, yet he was afraid what the work would come to. It is very notable that when Christ rebukes Peter, he also checks the severity of the devil, tempting him to idolatry, and Peter's dissuading him from sufferings; it is spoken to both: "Get behind me, Satan." Our Lord has so strong an inclination to die for us that he looked upon carnal pity to his person with the same indignation and scorn that he does upon a temptation to idolatry. However, the condescension and tenderness of Christ to his erring disciple is to be observed. He does not merely rebuke him but instructs him—and the rest of his disciples. Thus can Christ make an advantage of our failings. Peter's carnal counsel was the occasion of this excellent lesson, which Christ by this means has forever consigned to the use and profit of the church: "If any person will come after me, let him deny himself."

I shall open these words. Christ says, "If anyone" to show that the duty is of an unlimited concern. It involves all, whosoever will enter themselves in Christ's school or list themselves in his flock or company; it does not only concern a few who are called out to be champions for his cause and to expose their bodies to the cruel flames, but "if any will come after me." The word "will" is emphatic; it notes the full purpose and consent of the will—whosoever is firmly resolved. "Come after me" as a student after his teacher, as a sheep after his shepherd, as a soldier after his commander. "Come after": It is a phrase proper to students. The phrase shows the necessity of the duty, unless you will be disclaimed as none of his followers. Here Christ gives us the main character of his own disciples. Christianity is a school of people who deny themselves and their own conveniences for Christ's sake.

"Let him deny himself": these are the words that I shall insist upon. And in them there are two things to be observed:

- The act: "Let him deny."
- The object: "himself."

1. For the act, the verb "to deny" is wholly emphatic; it means "Let him utterly deny himself." The concept of denial properly belongs to speeches, but by a metaphor it may be also applied to things. To speeches it is proper, as to propositions

or requests. In propositions we are said to deny when we contradict that which is affirmed; in requests we deny when we refuse to grant what is desired of us. Now by an easy translation it may also be applied to things, which we are said to deny when we neglect, slight, or oppose them; as denying the power of godliness, neglecting or opposing it. With propriety enough the word may retain its original sense, because all things are managed in the heart of man by rational debates, counsels, and suggestions, and we are said to deny when we refuse to give assent to fleshly dictates and counsels. The flesh, or our corrupt self, has its inclinations, its motions in the soul. It speaks to us by our own thoughts and puts us upon this or that work. Envy, lust, and corrupt inclinations have a voice, and an authoritative voice too, that grace is quite apt to give a strong negative. Envy bids Cain, "Go kill your brother." Ambition bids Absalom, "Rebel against your father." Covetousness bids Judas, "Betray your Lord and master." In the same way, worldly affection bids us, "Pursue present things with all your might." Now because we are wedded to our opinions, and these are the suggestions of our own hearts, therefore they are called self; and we are said to deny when we enter our dissent and deny the motion. Flesh, what have I to do with you? I am not "a debtor to the flesh." I will hazard all for Christ and make it my work to get into covenant with God. This for the act: "Let him deny."

2. The object is the next word to be opened: "himself." It is an expansive word which does not only involve our persons but whatever is ours—so far as it stands in opposition to God or comes in competition to him. It is a word that refers to a person and all his lusts, a person and all his relations, a person and all his interests. Life, and all the appendages of life, is one aggregate thing that in Scripture is called "self." In short, whatever is of oneself, in oneself, belonging to oneself—as a corrupt or carnal person—all that is to be denied. And indeed

every person has many a self within himself; his lusts are himself; his life is himself; his name is himself; his wealth, liberty, ease, favor, property, father, mother, and all relations—they are included within the term of "self." As when our Lord explains it, "If anyone will come after me, and not hate his father and mother, and wife and children, and brothers and sisters, and even his own life, he cannot be my disciple." The word "to hate" is the same as denying or neglecting his duty to them for God's sake, when a higher duty is to take place. I admit, though, among the things that are called "self," there is a difference.

Firstly, some are absolutely evil and must be denied without limitation. These are like lusts and carnal affections, which are very properly called self, because we are as tender to them as of our own souls; and therefore they are expressed by the terms of the "right hand" and the "right eye." A sinner will as soon part with his eyes as with his lusts or the pleasure of his senses. And so they are called "members": "Mortify your members, which are on the earth." Sin is riveted in the soul, and it is as irksome to a natural heart to part with any lust as with a member or joint of the body; we are willing to hold them by as fast and as close as we hold ourselves; we startle at a reproof, as if a joint were pricked or touched.

Secondly, other things are only evil respectively, as they prove idols or snares to us. This includes things like life and all the ornaments, comforts, and conveniences of life or liberty, honors, wealth, friends, health—they are all called "self." The reason is because by love, which is the affection of union, they are incorporated into us and become parts of us: "Ephraim is joined to idols." They are cemented with them. Now that which is to be denied in these things is not so much the thing itself, but our corruption that mingles with them and causes them to become a snare to the soul.

The point that I shall insist on out of the whole is the following doctrine: It is the duty of all who would be Christ's disciples to deny themselves.

I shall handle the doctrine of self-denial

1. In general.
2. In its several kinds and subjective parts.

First, in general. In managing this argument, I shall use the following method: 1. Give the extent of self-denial. 2. The reasons of this duty, with the most effectual motives and arguments of persuasion. 3. The signs by which we may know whether we omit or practice it. 4. The helps that the Scripture prescribes for our furtherance in so great a work.

The extent of self-denial. As a foundation for all the rest, I shall first consider the extent of the duty of self-denial, both in regard of the object, or the things that are to be denied, and in regard of the subject, or the persons who are to practice it.

For the object: As for a person's own self, it is a bundle of idols. When God was laid aside, self succeeded to the crown; we set up everything that we call our own. Everything before which we may put that possessive "ours" is able to be abused and set up as a snare, which includes all the excellences and comforts of human life: both inward and outward.

For the understanding of this, and that you may know how far self is to be denied, I must provide some general considerations, and then give some particulars. This is because it seems harsh and contrary to reason that a person should deny himself, since nature teaches a person to love himself and cherish himself: "No person ever hated his own flesh," and grace does not disallow it.

1. Therefore, in general, you must know when respecting yourself is blameworthy. There is a lawful self-love: "You shall love your neighbor as yourself." In this there is not

only a direction to love our neighbor but a concession and allowance implied to love ourselves; and in so doing we do well. By an innocent and natural respect nature fortifies itself and seeks its own preservation. A person may respect himself in a regular way. But that self which we must hate or deny is the one that stands in opposition to God or competition with him—and so jostles with him for the throne. Lay aside God, and self steps in as the next heir. It is the great idol of the world, ever since the Fall, that when people are so bold as to depose God, self succeeds in the throne. Fallen man, like Reuben, takes over his father's bed. Self intercepted all those respects and embraces that were due to God himself, and so man became both his own idol and an idolater. It is with God and self as it was with Dagon and the ark; they can never stand together in competition. Set up the ark, and Dagon must fall upon his face. Set up Dagon, and the ark is deposed and put down. Well then, if we would know when self is sinfully respected, we must consider what are the rights and the undoubted flowers of the crown of heaven.

I mean, what are those special privileges and respects that are so appropriated to the Godhead as that they cannot without treason to the King of all the earth be alienated from him or communicated to any creature? Now these are four:

(i.) To be the first cause, upon whom all things depend in their being and operation.

(ii.) To be the chiefest good, and therefore to be valued above all beings, interests, and concerns in the world.

(iii.) To be the highest lord and most absolute sovereign, who sways all things by his laws and providence.

(iv.) To be the last end, in which all things do at length terminate and center upon.

Firstly, God is the first cause, so he would keep up the respects of the world to his majesty by dependence and trust. Now it is the ambition of man to affect an independency, to be a god to himself, sufficient for his own happiness. Our first parents greedily grabbed at that bait: "You shall be as gods." The devil meant it not in a blessed conformity, but a cursed self-sufficiency; and we are all apt to be taken in the same snare, which certainly is a very grievous sin. Nothing can be more hateful to God. This therefore is a great part of self-denial, to work us off from other dependences and to trust in God alone.

Secondly, as God is the chiefest good, so he must have the highest esteem. Valuing other things above God is the ground of all bankruptcy in the business of religion. When anything is honored above God, or made equal with God, or indulged against the will of God, Dagon is set up, and the ark is made to fall.

Thirdly, as God is the highest lord and most absolute sovereign, it is his peculiar prerogative to give laws to the creature. Therefore self is not to interpose and give laws to us, but only God; his will must stand. The great contest indeed between God and the creature is: Whose will shall stand, God's will or ours? Who shall give laws to us, self or God? Fleshly nature sets up laws against laws, and our fleshly wills set up providence against providence. Self-will is revealed by murmuring against God's providence, by rebellion against his laws, and will give homage and obedience to self: "We will walk in the way of our own heart." "Whatever comes out of our mouths, that we will do." So the apostle makes it to be the root of all sin when a person is drawn away by his own lusts and his own will, which is set up against the laws of God. So in providence, a stubborn creature will not submit when God's will is declared. It was a great submission and an act of self-denial on Christ's part when he said:

"Not as I will, but as you will." But self says, "Not as you will, but as I will." We, by murmuring, set up an anti-providence against God.

Fourthly, as God is the last end of our beings and actions, the supreme cause is to be the utmost end: "God made all things for himself." But now in all that we do we look to ourselves; vain man sets up self at the end of every action and jostles out God. All the actions of life are but a kind of homage to the idol of self. If men eat and drink, it is to nourish self, a meat-offering and drink-offering to appetite. If they pray or praise, it is but to worship self, to advance the status of self. If they give alms, they are a sacrifice offered to the idol of self-esteem. "They give alms to be seen by man," Christ says. When this happens, self is set up, and God is deposed.

2. Now let me give you some particular examples: moral or natural and civil excellencies. So for moral excellencies: Righteousness is apt to be a snare in a point of self-dependence. Paul found it to be "a loss," a hindrance from casting ourselves entirely upon grace. It is the highest point of self-denial for a person to deny his own righteousness, to see the dung and dross that is in himself and in all his moral excellencies. So also, concerning our own wisdom, that is a self that comes to be denied. It is said to Babylon: "Your understanding has undone you." So of all people, when we presume upon our own sense and apprehension, we soon go wrong. This is the main thing to be considered here. For Peter, out of carnal wisdom, dissuades Christ, and then Christ says, "Whoever will come after me, let him deny himself," that is, deny the dictates of his own reason and will. He who makes his own heart his oracle asks the counsel of a fool. We shall be complaining and disputing till we have disputed ourselves out of all religion: "Cause me to understand where I have erred." Until we come to see by the divine

light, carnal wisdom is always making lies and giving ill reports of religion. We think it folly and preciseness to be strict, and that zeal is fury, and it is cowardice and disgrace to put up wrong. We shall still be calling good evil, and evil good, because we are wise in our own eyes; there is a woe pronounced upon such: "Woe unto them who are wise in their own eyes, and prudent in their own sight!" It is an excellent point of self-denial to "become a fool, that we may be wise." As when we squint with our eyes so that we may see more clearly, so we must put out the eye of carnal wisdom and become fools, so that we may be wise for Christ.

So also for all civil interests: Life is the most precious possession of the creature, and yet it is not too good to be denied: Christ says this: "Whosoever shall lose his life for my sake shall find it." That is the gospel-way of living well: to lose all for God. And we should deny these things, not only in purpose and vow but when it comes to trial. As it is said of the saints: "They loved not their lives to the death." When it comes to a point, either they must leave their God or lose their lives on the account of religion. The loving-kindness of God is better than life.

So for material possessions: "We have left all and followed you," say the disciples. We must leave our coat, as Joseph did, so that we may keep our conscience.

So also for fame and esteem in the world. Even though to a person of respect this is exceedingly precious, yet John the Baptist says of Christ: "He must increase, but I must decrease." We must be content to be nobodys who Christ may rise up into the greater sum. We must be as one in a crowd who holds up another person on his shoulders: We are lost in the throng, but the other is able to be seen by all.

So for our friends: "Whoever does not hate his father and his mother . . ." There are times when we are to deny our friends, as, suppose, when we shall incur their displeasure out of faithfulness to Christ. Carnal parents may frown upon us, and maybe even refrain from giving us provision and other conveniences of life. But it is better for an earthly father to frown than for God to do so, since God will make it up to us in spiritual family members.

So also for being just and doing right: We must not own father, mother, brothers, or sisters, for this is but more handsome and natural bribery. Levi was commended for this by the Lord: "The one who says to his father and mother, 'I have not seen him'," neither did he acknowledge his brothers, nor know his own children, but observed my word." It is good to be blind and deaf to all relations in this case. Asa did not spare his own mother but deposed her since she was idolatrous.

> "If your brother, the son of your mother, or your son, or your daughter, or the wife of your flesh, or your friend, who is as your own soul, entice you secretly, saying, 'Let us go serve other gods that you have not known' . . . you shall not give consent to him, nor hearken unto him; neither shall your eye pity him; neither shall you spare, neither shall you conceal him; but you shall surely kill him; your hand shall be first upon him to put him to death, and afterward the hand of all the people."

We are apt to look upon these rules as intended for Utopia and have but a theoretical knowledge of them.

So also for carnal things: If it is a right hand or a right eye, it must be plucked out and cut off. If it is as gainful and as profitable a sin as the right hand is profitable to us, yet it must not be spared: "We must deny all ungodliness," though ever so pleasing.

Thus for the object, it extends to all things. For the subject: See the extent of it, for it reaches all sorts of people. Christ says, "If anyone will come after me, he must deny himself." The specific circumstances of this passage in Mark are notable when Christ gives the lesson of self-denial: "When he had called the people unto him, with his disciples also, he said unto them, 'Whoever will come after me, let him deny himself.'" There is no calling, no sex, no age, no duty, no condition of life that is excluded; but one way or other, they are put upon self-denial. No calling: Magistrates and those who are called to public trust are most obliged, in regard of God and people, to deny themselves. The self-denial of Joseph is notable: Though he was a great officer in Egypt, yet his family ran the same lot with other tribes. Also with Joshua in the division of the land: He took his own lot and share last. People in public places are most liable to mind private interest, to the neglect of the public; but they ought not to feather their nests with public spoils.

So also for people who are not in the public eye: It is not the duty of public persons only; all people are liable to self-seeking. Many times your private callings may be against the public interest, either of religion or civil welfare, as they who made shrines for Diana when the gospel came, and reformation likely to be wrought. They cried, "Our gain will be gone." Therefore in this case you should be content to sink and to suffer loss, as the lighter elements descend to conserve the universe. Or it may be that you have thrived financially due to iniquity; now you are to deny yourselves by making restitution. Zacchaeus says: "I will restore four-fold, and give to the poor." Restitution is a hard duty, but a necessary one; and you must vomit up your sweet morsels with which you have glutted yourself, or else your conscience will not be healthy.

And so for other callings and relations, particularly ministers. Ministers, of all people, have the most need to practice this duty. We are to deny our own ends. How many carnal ends may a man promote by his service in the ministry? Fame, applause, and the satisfying of our necessity. However, we are not to preach ourselves, but Christ Jesus the Lord. We are to deny ourselves in our learning; we are debtors to the learned and unlearned. We are to become all things to all, and it is certain that Christ has lambs as well as sheep. We must be content to go back ten degrees, so that we may speak plainly to all, not to soar aloft in speculation. Such is more for our fame and repute of learning, but less for profit.

So for people: In hearing you must deny the curiosity of the ear, that others may profit by plainer lessons and that every one may have his portion in due season. It is a great part of self-denial to suffer the words of exhortation. Guilt is apt to recoil when tender parts are touched. Now you are to deny yourselves, to love the reproof as well as the comfort, and count it precious oil. Consider the submission that was in Hezekiah when the prophet came with the bitter threatening of a curse that should cleave to his posterity: "Good is the word of the Lord," a sweet submission of a sanctified judgment.

So also for all genders: It is a duty not only for men but for women also. They are to deny themselves in their delicacies of life, that they may exercise themselves in the grave duties of religion.

It is necessary also in all duties, especially those two great duties that divide and encompass the whole Christian life: prayer and praise. Both of them should be practiced with self-denial. When we come for grace, we should deny our own merit: O Lord, not for our own righteousness. And when grace is received—when we come to praise God—self must vanish, so that God may have all the praise. When the good servant gives an account of his faithfulness, he says, "Not my doing, but your pound has gained ten pounds"; he gives it all to grace. So the apostle Paul checks himself, as if he had spoken unbecoming of himself: "I labored more than you all, yet not I, but the grace of God that was with me." So also elsewhere the apostle says, "I live," then quickly draws in his words again, "not I, but Christ lives in me." As the elders throw their crowns at the Lamb's feet, so all our excellencies must be laid at the feet of Christ. As the stars disappear when the sun arises, so we must shrink into nothing in our own thoughts. When Joab had conquered Rabbah, he sent for David to take the garland of honor; so when we have done anything by grace, we must send for Christ to take the honor. Prayer is the humble appeal to mercy, disclaiming merit; and praise is the setting of the crown upon Christ's head: not I, but the grace of God that is wrought in me.

To apply this, all people are to practice this duty—in all things, at all times, and with all their hearts. Firstly, all people are to practice it. Oh, do not put it off to others; no person can exempt himself. Usually when these duties are pressed, we think they are intended for people in great places and for people who are very powerful. But it is a duty that lies upon all, since all are apt to seek themselves. When Christ spoke something concerning Peter, it is said: "Peter looked about on the disciple Jesus loved." So we are apt to look about to others. Look for it, because before you die you will be eminently called to this service. Never did a Christian go out of this world but one time or other God tried him in some eminent point of self-denial. As it is said, God tempted Abraham and tried him in that difficult point of offering his son. So Christ also tested the young man: "Go, sell all that you have, and give to the poor."

Secondly, for the object: in all things. Do not let your self-denial be partial and halfhearted, as Saul killed some of the cattle but spared the fat, as well as Agag. Many can deny themselves in many things, but they are loath to give up all to God without limits and reservations. As Joshua deposed all the kings of Canaan, so every lust is to be cast out of the throne. The one who denies himself only in some things denies himself in none. Jehu put Baal's priests to death but continued the calves in Dan and Bethel out of interest and reasons of state. Herod denied himself in many things but could not part with his Herodias.

Thirdly, you must deny yourself always. It must not be temporary and occasional. When we are in a good mood we can give up and renounce all and be humble and ascribe all to grace. And we may hang our head for a day. But there should be a constant sense of our unworthiness kept up, and a purpose of renouncing all and giving up all. It is not enough to deny a person's self in a thing wherein there is no pleasure and when his soul abhors dainty food, but it must be in things that are desirable. This must be constantly practiced, too. Even Ahab humbled himself for a few days.

Lastly, it must be with all our heart. Which signifies that it must not be done by a mere constraint of providence, as a mariner in a storm casts away his goods by force. Rather it should be as a bride leaves her father's house, no more returning: "Forget your father's house." Your self-denial must be out of a principle of grace and out of love to Christ. And you must not do it casually, but with your whole heart. There is no such great self-seeking as is carried on usually under the color of self-denial. The devil disguises himself into all forms and shapes. As Jacob put on Esau's clothes so that he might appear rough and hairy—and so get the blessing—so many seem to deny themselves of the comforts of life, but it is only for their own praise. The Pharisees were liberal in alms; they denied themselves in giving, which others could not do. But they did it to be seen by others. Therefore this self-denial must not be self-seeking, carried on under pretense, for that is abominable to God.

APPENDIX A
MANTON'S LEGACY: PURITAN, PREACHER, PUBLIC THEOLOGIAN

> There is not a poor discourse in the whole collection [of Manton's works]—they are evenly good, constantly excellent. Ministers who do not know Manton need not wonder if they are themselves unknown.
>
> C. H. Spurgeon

> [Thomas Manton] is easily the prince among the divines of the Puritan school.
>
> J. C. Ryle

Introduction

Thomas Manton's complete works were first published in 1870 by the London printer James Nisbet. The decision to publish the works of an otherwise unknown Puritan divine 200 years after his death indicates renewed interest in Puritan figures during the latter half of the nineteenth century in England. The preface to this publication by the Bishop of Liverpool, J. C. Ryle (1816–1900), begins, not surprisingly, by noting Manton's general obscurity in England at that time.

> The publication of a complete and uniform edition of Manton's works is a great boon to the readers of English theology.

Many of his best writings have been hitherto inaccessible to all who have not long purses and large libraries. The few who know him would gladly testify, I am sure, that Thomas Manton was one of the best authors of his day, and that his works richly deserve reprinting.

As noted in a previous chapter, Manton's writings drew their chief clientele from Puritans in Britain and colonial America. Especially after the Act of Uniformity in 1662, Puritans like Manton experienced a precipitous decline of favor and support. The popularity of Puritan thought during the 1640s and 1650s, in fact, was only countered by a spate of legislative opposition in the 1660s that by all accounts silenced the Puritan cause in England—Manton included. Carl Trueman explains:

> The Great Ejection of 1662 effectively removed from the Church, and thus from the intellectual establishment, the vast majority of those ministers committed to a more thoroughly Reformed faith; it therefore surrendered both the Church and, as a result, the academy to a group whose theological concerns were generally more latitudinarian.

Puritan, Preacher, Public Theologian

As a result of the sweeping changes underway both politically and theologically in the 1660s, it is not surprising that Thomas Manton's writings did not find the reception that they might otherwise have experienced. Indeed, the marginalization of Puritan thought subsequent to the Restoration was sweeping and severe. It is for this reason, in fact, that J. C. Ryle's preface to the first completed edition of Manton's corpus devotes itself almost entirely to defending the importance of Manton's work given that he was considered a "Puritan." An extended quote from Ryle's preface illustrates his defense.

Let me clear the way by considering an objection which is frequently brought against Manton and other divines of his school. That objection is that he was a "Puritan." I admit the fact, and do not deny it for a moment. A friend and associate of Baxter, Calamy, Owen, and Bates—a leading man in all the fruitless conferences between Puritans and Churchmen in the early part of Charles II's reign—ejected from St. Paul's, Covent Garden, by the disgraceful Act of Uniformity—a sufferer even into bonds on account of his Nonconformist opinions,—if ever there was an English divine who must be classed as a Puritan, that man is Dr Manton. But what of it, if he was a Puritan? It does not prove that he was not a valuable theologian, an admirable writer, and an excellent man. Let me once for all make a few plain statements about the school to which Manton belonged—the school of the English Puritans. It is one of those points of ecclesiastical history of our country about which the ignorance of most Englishmen is deep and astounding. There are more baseless and false ideas current about them than any about any class of men in British history. The impressions of most people are so ridiculously incorrect that one could laugh if the subject were not so serious. To hear them talk about Puritans is simply ludicrous. They make assertions which prove either that they know nothing at all of what they are talking about, or that they have forgotten the ninth commandment [against bearing false witness]. For Dr Manton's sake, and for the honor of a cruelly misrepresented body of men, let me try to explain to the reader what the Puritans really were. He that supposes that they were ignorant, fanatical sectaries, haters of the Crown of England—men alike destitute of learning, holiness, or loyalty—has got a great deal to learn.

More than 125 years have passed since Ryle penned these prefatory remarks to Manton's completed works. Since that time many studies have disproven some of the caricatures

associated with Puritans like Manton, but the general opprobrium of the term *Puritanism* remains.

This raises the question of whether this term is the best
descriptor of Manton as a person. Manton does not truly
embody any of the characteristics that Ryle mentions. He
was neither ignorant nor fanatical, but was a man of peace.
Nor was he a "hater of the Crown of England." On the
contrary, Manton sternly opposed the execution of Charles
I, and he was instrumental in the restoration of Charles II.
Finally, Manton was certainly not "destitute of learning,
holiness, or loyalty." In regard to learning, he earned his
BA, BD, and DD from Oxford; as for holiness, he was highly
regarded by conformists and nonconformists alike; and as
far as loyalty is concerned, Manton dedicated the entirety
of his midcareer toward comprehension within the Church
of England. His great desire was for the church to be one
and for the English nation to be holy and united.

If these are the characteristics of a Puritan, therefore,
they certainly do not apply to Manton. Nevertheless, this
book maintains that Manton should still be considered a
Puritan—given that the term *Puritan*, of course, is expanded
to account for Manton's broadness in thinking in regard to
exegetical, theological, and political issues. Indeed, as a
recent book by Carl Trueman on John Owen testifies, the
English Puritans are perhaps described well as "Reformed
Catholic." Although they were certainly Reformed in their
theological and biblical thinking, they were catholic or ecumenical in regard to their sources; and they differed on any
number of other issues, whether social, economic, or political. The term *Puritan* is a broad one, in other words, that
includes pastors and theologians like Thomas Manton.

The second way to describe Manton is by using the more
concrete terms *pastor* or *preacher*. As a Reformed Puritan
pastor, Manton's principal task was to exposit God's word

each week by preaching a biblical sermon that simultaneously explained the original meaning of whatever passage
he was expounding and connected its historical significance
to the practical realities of the Christian life. Both parts
were essential, and both are clearly apparent in all of Manton's sermons. The explication was intended for thinking,
while the application was intended for doing.

Manton, for his part, was well known for being an excellent preacher—indeed, "the king of preachers," as one
contemporary noted. As a preacher he dealt with the problems in England in the most effective way he could: by
spiritually indicting the English nation and by suggesting
repair of social and political unrest by means of national
moral reform. Specifically, Manton did this in three ways:
first, through the sermons he preached at Parliament; second, through his continued leadership in the classis movement to establish presbyterianism; and third, through his
sermons and lectures to his congregations at Stoke Newington and later at Covent Garden.

To address pubic concerns by means of sermons was
potentially difficult for a Puritan pastor such as Manton.
This is due to the established exegetical practices of
Reformed commentators in the line of William Perkins and
John Calvin, whose primary concern when preaching or
lecturing was expounding the intention of the author. The
reticence on the part of Reformed exegetes to step outside
the biblical text determines in part why Manton dealt with
social issues only indirectly. It would be wrong to conclude,
however, that Manton was not interested in addressing
national concerns. He certainly was. But as a Reformed
pastor he dealt with national issues only when, in his view,
the text of this or that passage lent itself legitimately to such
issues—and more often than not, it did, since God's word
speaks to all cultures at all times.

In addition to characterizing Manton as a Puritan and as a preacher or pastor, there is one final way to describe Manton: public theologian. In contrast to the more historical term *Puritan*, the phrase *public theologian* is certainly a modern one. According to contemporary scholar Ron Thiemann, who authored a book with this title, public theology is

> faith seeking to understand the relation between Christian convictions and the broader social and cultural context within which the Christian community lives.

Although Thiemann's definition presupposes a clear separation of church and state, which was certainly not the case in seventeenth-century England, this term does suggest itself as an apt description of Manton's life in general and his works in particular.

This is because Manton lived his life precariously between his "Christian convictions" as an ordained minister in the Anglican Church and the "social and cultural context" of seventeenth-century England. Another lengthy quote from J. C. Ryle indicates this:

> In an age like this, Manton occupied for several years a very prominent position. He was not a country parson, living scores of miles from London, and absorbed in unobtrusive pastoral labors among a rural population. On the contrary, he was a standard-bearer in the forefront of the battle . . . a man who could neither say, nor do, nor write anything without being observed. Did Oliver Cromwell require a minister to offer up prayer at the public ceremony of his undertaking the Protectorship? Manton was the minister. Did the Long Parliament want a special sermon preached before its members on that great public event? Manton was frequently ordered to be the preacher. Did

the famous Westminster Assembly want a commendatory preface written to their Confession and Catechisms of worldwide reputation? They commit the execution of it to the pen of Thomas Manton. Was a Committee of Triers appointed to examine persons who were to be admitted into the ministry or inducted into livings? Manton was a leading member of this committee. Was a movement made by the Presbyterian divines, after Cromwell's death, to restore the monarchy and bring back Charles II? Manton was a leader in the movement. Was an effort made after the Restoration to bring about a reconciliation between the Episcopal Church and the Nonconformists? Manton was one of the commissioners to act in the matter in the unhappy Savoy Conference. In short, if there was one name which more than another was incessantly before the public for several years about the period of the Restoration, that name was Manton's. If there was one divine who, willingly or unwillingly, was constantly standing under the full gaze of friends and foes in London, that divine was the Rector of St. Paul's, Covent Garden, Thomas Manton.

Manton lived an extremely public life. For him, the division between church and state was negligible. His role as a minister in the Church of England related just as much to the "Church" as to "England." His sermons were thus truly an English enterprise that sought to apply what Manton regarded as the practical truths of God's word to Englishmen and Englishwomen alike. He sought to remedy the social and religious ills of the English nation in the most "practical" way he could do so: by applying God's word to a nation that so desperately needed to hear it. As it turns out, the English nation did not receive Manton's sermons in any substantial way, as the momentous changes the nation experienced during the "decisive decades" of 1640–60 ended poorly for Puritans like Manton. Although this collective marginalization of Puritans has totally obscured the life and works of people like Thomas Manton, it is hoped that future studies will reconsider the contribution that this Puritan pastor made at a truly decisive time in the history of the church. It is likewise hoped that readers will be encouraged to begin reading Manton's own works and that they will see for themselves how much this Puritan pastor is able to contribute to the church.

APPENDIX B
MANTON'S WORKS: A GUIDE FOR FUTURE READING

The few who know him would gladly testify, I am sure, that
Thomas Manton was one of the best authors of his day.

J. C. Ryle

Introduction

The purpose of this book has been to introduce readers
to Thomas Manton, the Puritan pastor. Although this book
comes to an end at the conclusion of this appendix, the
journey of interacting with Manton does not have to conclude. Indeed, it is hoped that this book has whetted the
appetite of many, so that they will begin reading Manton's
own works for themselves. For those who would like to read
more of Manton's sermons, this brief appendix includes a
list of many of the sermons that Manton preached, which
are included in the twenty-two volumes of his works.

As has been explained in this book, practically all of
Manton's works are sermons. He was, after all, a pastor, and
a Reformed one at that, which meant that he devoted much
of his energy to preaching biblical sermons. Some of these
sermons became extended sermon series, some became biblical commentaries, some were preached before Parliament
or in prison, and some were preached independently for fast

days or for preparation of the sacraments. Regardless of the exact circumstance, they all offer wonderful examples of Puritan sermons—which are known for depth, doctrine, practicality, and vibrant imagery.

Manton's Works

For those who would like to read some of Manton's works but are not exactly sure where to begin, the list below contains some of his more famous works. Many theological libraries contain Manton's twenty-two-volume corpus; so these works are readily accessible. Better yet, many of his works can be read online for free (www.newblehome.co.uk/manton is just one example). Some readers might want to only consult Manton on passages that they are teaching, which will certainly help them think more closely about the passage; others may be reading through the Bible and need some explanation (both biblical and pastoral); others just may need some encouragement, which they will doubtlessly get as they read through Manton's various works. Whatever exact situation different readers find themselves in, it is hoped that this book has offered a reliable and helpful guide to Thomas Manton's life and works, and it is especially hoped that readers will be willing to read Manton's works for themselves and, by so doing, receive inspiration, explanation, and clarity.

List of Major Works in Manton's 22-volume Corpus[1]

Volume 1
- *An Estimate of Manton* by J. C. Ryle
- *Memoir* by William Harris
- *A Practical Exposition of the Lord's Prayer*

---

1. Thomas Manton, *The Works of Thomas Manton*, 22 vols. (London: Nisbet, 1870 ; Worthington, PA: Maranatha Publications, 1900).

- *The Temptation and Transfiguration of Christ*
- *Christ's Redemption and Eternal Existence*

Volume 2
- *Sermons on Various Texts*
- *Farewell Sermon Following the Act of Uniformity*
- *Funeral Sermon Following the Execution of the Rev. Christopher Love*

Volume 3
- *Sermons on 2 Thessalonians 2*
- *A Practical Exposition of Isaiah 53*

Volume 4
- *A Practical Exposition of James*

Volume 5
- *A Practical Exposition of Jude*
- *Two Sermons Preached before the House of Commons*
- *Four Sermons Preached at the Cripplegate Morning Exercises*
- *Manton's Preface to* Smectymnuus Redivivus

Volume 6
- *Sermons on Psalm 119:1–46*

Volume 7
- *Sermons on Psalm 119:47–98*

Volume 8
- *Sermons on Psalm 119:98–141*

Volume 9
- *Sermons on Psalm 119:141–150*
- *Sermons on Matthew 25*

Volume 10
- *Sermons on Matthew 25*
- *Sermons on John 17*

Volume 11
- *Sermons on John 17*
- *Sermons on Romans 6*
- *Sermons on Romans 8*

Volume 12
- *Sermons on Romans 8*
- *Sermons on 2 Corinthians 5*

Volume 13
- *Sermons on 2 Corinthians 5*
- *Sermons on Hebrews 11*

Volume 14
- *Sermons on Hebrews 11*

Volume 15
- *Sermons on Hebrews 11*
- *A Treatise on the Life of Faith*
- *A Treatise on Self-Denial*
- *Several Sermons Preached on Public Occasions*

Volume 16
- *Sermons on Several Texts of Scripture*
- *Sermons on Titus 2:11–14; Hebrews 6:18; John 14:1; Luke 12:48; Mark 10:17–27*

Volume 17
- *Sermons on Several Texts of Scripture, Part 1*

- *Mark 10:17–27; 2 Thessalonians 1:3; Mark 3:5; Genesis 24:63*
- *Sermons on Several Texts of Scripture, Part 2*
- *Several Sermons: Luke 16:30–31; Acts 24:14–16; 1 Thessalonians 5:16–17*

Volume 18
- *Sermons on Several Texts of Scripture*
- *Forty-five Sermons on Various Texts: Isaiah 50:10; Luke 2:52; Philippians 2:7*

Volume 19
- *Sermons on Several Texts of Scripture*
- *Ecclesiastes; Leviticus*
- *Series of Sermons on Ephesians 5:1–27*

Volume 20
- *Sermons on Several Texts of Scripture*
- *Series of Sermons: Philippians 3:1–21; 2 Thessalonians 1; 1 John 2:12–14; 1 John 3*

Volume 21
- *Series of Sermons on 1 John 3*
- *Sermons on Several Texts of Scripture*
- *Acts 2:37, 38; 1 Peter 1:23; Psalm 19:13; Psalm 131; Ezekiel 18:23*

Volume 22
- *Sermons on Several Texts of Scripture*
- *Funeral Sermon Preached upon the Death of Dr. Manton by Dr. William Bates*
- *Index of Subjects*
- *Index of Texts*
- *Index of Principal Texts*

BIBLIOGRAPHY

Primary Sources

Barlow, Thomas. *De Studio Theologiae: Or, Directions for the Choice of Books in the Study of Divinity.* Oxford: William Offley, 1699.

Baxter, Richard. *The Autobiography of Richard Baxter.* Edited by N. H. Keeble. London: J. M. Dent and Sons, Ltd., 1974.

Calvin, John. *Commentaries on the Catholic Epistles.* Edited by John Owen. Grand Rapids: Eerdmans, 1948.

Dickson, David. *An exposition of all St. Paul's epistles together with an explanation of those other epistles of the apostles St. James, Peter, John and Jude: wherein the sense of every chapter and verse is analytically unfolded and the text enlightened.* London: R.I., 1659.

Hemingsen, Niels. *A learned and fruitefull commentarie vpon the Epistle of Iames the Apostle wherein are diligently and profitably entreated all such matters and chiefe commonplaces of religion as are touched in the same epistle.* London: John Kingston, 1577.

Leigh, Edward. *Annotations upon all the New Testament philologicall and theologicall wherein the emphasis and elegancie of the Greeke is observed, some imperfections in our translation are discovered, divers Jewish rites and customes tending to illustrate the text are mentioned, many antilogies and seeming contradictions reconciled, severall darke and obscure places opened, sundry passages vindicated from the false glosses of papists and hereticks.* London: W.W. and E.E., 1650.

Luther, Martin. "Preface to the Epistles of St. James and St. Jude." In *Luther's Works*, vol. 35. Edited by Abdel Wentz. Philadelphia: Muhlenberg Press, 1960.

——————. "Prefaces to the New Testament." In *Luther's Works*, vol. 35. Edited by Theodore Bachmann. Philadelphia: Muhlenberg Press, 1960.

Manton, Thomas. *The Works of Thomas Manton.* 22 vols. London: Nisbet, 1870; Worthington, PA: Maranatha Publications, 1900.

Mayer, John. *Ecclesiastica interpretatio: or The expositions upon the difficult and doubtful passages of the seven Epistles called catholike, and the*

Revelation Collected out of the best esteemed, both old and new writers, together with the authors examinations, determinations, and short annotations. The texts in the seven Epistles of Iames, Peter, Iohn and Iude are six and forty. The expositions upon the Revelation are set forth by way of question and answer. Here is also a briefe commentary upon every verse of each chapter, setting forth the coherence and sense, and the authors, and time of writing every of these bookes. London: John Haviland, 1627.

—————. *Praxis theologica: or, The Epistle of the Apostle St Iames resolued, expounded, and preached vpon by way of doctrine and vse for the benefit and instruction of all Christian people, and for the helpe and direction of yong practisers in theology. To which is added an alphabeticall table of the distinct doctrines heere handled, beeing a great part of the whole body of doctrines arising out of the holy Scriptures.* London: John Beale, 1629.

Pemble, William. *Vindiciae Fidei: Or, a Treatise of Justification by Faith.* Oxford, 1625. Reprint, Edinburgh: The Banner of Truth Trust, 2002.

Perkins, William. *The Art of Prophesying.* Edinburgh: The Banner of Truth Trust, 1996.

Piscator, Johannes. *Analysis logica septem epistolarum Apostolicarum, quae catholicae appellari solent videlicet Jacobi I. Petri II. Johannis III. Judae I. Una cum scholiis et observationibus locorum doctrinae.* London: Johan. Wolfe, 1593.

Poole, Matthew. *Annotations on the Holy Bible.* 2 vols. London, 1683–85. Reprint, London: Banner of Truth Trust, 1962.

Thoresby, Ralph. *The Diary of Ralph Thoresby,* F.R.S. Vol. 1. London: Henry Colburn & Richard Bentley, 1860.

Turnbull, Richard. *An exposition upon the canonical epistle of Saint Iames: with the Tables, Analysis, and resolution, both of the whole Epistle, and of every Chapter thereof: with the particular resolution of every singular place.* London: John Windet, 1591.

Usher, James. *The Reduction of the Episcopacie unto the form of Synodical Government received in the Ancient Church.* London: T.N., 1656.

Vio, Tommaso de (Cajetan). *Opera omnia quotquot in sacrae Scripturae expositionem reperiuntur.* 5 vols. Lyons, 1639. Reprint, Hildesheim, Germany: Georg Olms Verlag, 2005.

Westminster Confession of Faith. London: E.M., 1658.

Wood, Anthony. *Athenae Oxonienses: an exact history of all the bishops who have had their education in the most ancient and famous University of Oxford, from the fifteenth year of King Henry to the seventeenth, Dom. 1500, to the end of the year 1690. To which are added, the fasti, or annals, of the said University, for the same time.* 2 vols. London: Half-Moon at St. Paul's Churchyard, 1691–92.

Whitby, Daniel. *A paraphrase and commentary upon all the epistles of the New Testament.* London: W. Bowyer, 1700.

Secondary Sources

Abernathy, George. *The English Presbyterians and the Stuart Restoration, 1648–1663*. Philadelphia: American Philosophical Society, 1965.

Bolam, C. G. *The English Presbyterians: From Elizabethan Puritanism to Moderate Unitarianism*. London: Allen and Unwin, 1968.

Bremer, Francis. *Congregational Communion: Clerical Friendship in the Anglo-American Puritan Community, 1610–1692*. Boston: Northeastern University Press, 1994.

—————. *Puritan Crisis: New England and the English Civil Wars, 1630–1670*. New York: Garland Publishing, 1989.

—————. *Shaping New Englands: Puritan Clergymen in Seventeenth-Century England and New England*. New York: Twayne, 1994.

Brodrick, George. *A History of the University of Oxford*. London: Longmans, Green, and Co., 1886.

Butler, Jon. *Awash in a Sea of Faith: Christianizing the American People*. Cambridge: Harvard University Press, 1990.

Clark, Peter. "The Ownership of Books in England, 1560–1640." In *Schooling and Society: Studies in the History of Education*. Edited by Lawrence Stone. Baltimore: The John Hopkins University Press, 1976.

Costello, William. *The Scholastic Curriculum at Early Seventeenth-Century Cambridge*. Cambridge: Harvard University Press, 1958.

Dictionary of National Biography. Edited by Leslie Stephen and Sidney Lee. Oxford: Oxford University Press, 1885–.

Feingold, Mordechai. "The Humanities." In *The History of the University of Oxford*, vol. 4. Edited by Nicholas Tyacke. Oxford: Oxford University Press, 1997, 211–358.

Harris, William. "Some Memoirs of the Life and Character of the Reverend and Learned Thomas Manton, D.D." In *The Complete Works of Thomas Manton*, vol. 1. London: Nisbet, 1870.

Hill, Christopher. *God's Englishman: Oliver Cromwell and the English Revolution*. New York: Harper and Row, 1970.

—————. *Puritanism and Revolution: Studies in Interpretation of the English Revolution of the Seventeenth Century*. London: Secker and Warburg, 1958.

—————. *Society and Puritanism in Pre-Revolutionary England*. London, Secker and Warburg, 1964.

Johnson, Luke T. "Letter of James." *Dictionary of Biblical Interpretation*. Edited by John Hayes. Nashville: Abingdon, 1999, 560–62.

—————. *The Letter of James*. New York: Doubleday, 1995.

Knapp, Henry. "Understanding the Mind of God: John Owen and Seventeenth-Century Exegetical Methodology." Ph.D. diss., Calvin Theological Seminary, 2002.

Lake, Peter. *Anglicans and Puritans? Presbyterianism and English Conformist Thought from Whitgift to Hooker.* London: Unwin Hyman, 1988.

Lotz, David. "Sola Scriptura: Luther on Biblical Authority." *Interpretation* 35 (1981): 273.

Mallet, Charles. *A History of the University of Oxford,* vol. 2. New York: Barnes and Noble, 1968.

Matthews, A. G. *Calamy Revised: Being a Revision of Edmund Calamy's Account of the Ministers and Others Ejected and Silenced, 1660–1662.* Oxford: Clarendon Press, 1988.

Muller, Richard. "Joseph Hall as Rhetor, Theologian, and Exegete: His Contribution to the History of Interpretation." In *Solomon's Divine Arts: Joseph Hall.* Edited by Gerald Sheppard. Cleveland: Pilgrim Press, 1991, 11–37.

—————. *Post-Reformation Reformed Dogmatics: The Rise and Development of Reformed Orthodoxy, ca. 1520 to ca. 1725.* 4 vols. Grand Rapids: Baker, 2003.

O'Day, Rosemary. *Education and Society 1500–1800: The Social Foundations of Education in Early Modern Britain.* New York: Longman, 1982.

—————. *English Clergy: The Emergence and Consolidation of a Profession 1558–1642.* Leicester University Press, 1979.

—————. *The Professions in Early Modern England, 1450–1800: Servants of the Commonweal.* London: Longman, 2000.

Oxford Dictionary of National Biography. Edited by H. G. Matthews and Brian Harrison. Oxford: Oxford University Press, 2004.

Porter, Stephen. "University and Society." *The History of the University of Oxford,* vol. 4. Edited by Nicholas Tyacke. Oxford: Oxford University Press, 1997, 25–104.

Richardson, Caroline. *English Preachers and Preaching 1640–1660: A Secular Study.* London: Society for Promoting Christian Knowledge, 1928.

Ryle, J. C. "An Estimate of Manton." In *The Works of Thomas Manton,* vol. 1. London: Nisbet, 1870.

Schnell, F. J. *Blundell's: A Short History of Famous West Country School.* London: Hutchinson, 1928.

Spurr, John. *English Puritanism 1603–1689.* New York: St. Martin's, 1998.

—————. *The Post-Reformation: Religion, Politics, and Society in Britain 1603–1714.* Harlow: Pearson Educational Limited, 2006.

—————. *The Restoration Church of England, 1646–1689.* New Haven: Yale University Press, 1991.

Stone, Lawrence. *Schooling and Society: Studies in the History of Education*. Baltimore: John Hopkins University Press, 1976.

———. "The Size and Composition of the Oxford Student Body 1580–1909." In *The University in Society*, vol. 1, *Oxford and Cambridge from the Fourteenth to the Early Nineteenth Century*. Edited by Lawrence Stone. Princeton: Princeton University Press, 1974.

———. *The University in Society*, vol. 1: *Oxford and Cambridge from the Fourteenth to the Early Nineteenth Century*. Princeton: Princeton University Press, 1974.

Thiemann, Ron. *Constructing a Public Theology: The Church in a Pluralistic Culture*. Louisville: John Knox Press, 1991.

Toon, Peter. *God's Statesman: The Life and Work of John Owen*. London: Paternoster, 1971.

Trueman, Carl. *The Claims of Truth: John Owen's Trinitarian Theology*. Carlisle: Paternoster Press, 1998.

———. *John Owen: Reformed Catholic, Renaissance Man*. Aldershot: Ashgate, 2007.

———. "Puritan Theology as Historical Event: A Linguistic Approach to the Ecumenical Context." In *Reformation and Scholasticism*. Edited by Willem van Asselt and Eef Dekker. Grand Rapids: Baker Academic, 2001, 253–76.

Trueman, Carl, and R. Scott Clark. *Protestant Scholasticism: Essays in Reassessment*. Carlisle: Paternoster Press, 1999.

Tyacke, Nicholas. *Aspects of English Protestantism c. 1530–1700*. Manchester: Manchester University Press, 2001.

———. *The History of the University of Oxford*, vol. 4. Oxford: Oxford University Press, 1997.

Watts, Michael. *The Dissenters: From the Reformation to the French Revolution*, vol. 1. Oxford: Clarendon Press, 1978.

Wood, Harold. *Church Unity without Uniformity: A Study of Seventeenth-century English Church Movements and of Richard Baxter's Proposals for a Comprehensive Church*. London: Epworth Press, 1963.

About the Illustrations

1.1 Portrait of Thomas Manton by Robert White. Line engraving by Robert White, published 1681. From the National Portrait Gallery, London.

1.2 Picture of Wadham College, Oxford, where Manton attended college during the late 1630s. From *Oxford and Its Colleges*, by J. Wells. Illustrated by Edmund New. London: London Methuen & Co, 1908. "The Garden Front Wadham College."

1.3 Portrait of King Charles I in 1648, who was taken prisoner during the English Civil War and beheaded for treason in 1649 by Parliament. From *A History of the American People*, by Woodrow Wilson, vol. 1. New York and London: Harper & Brothers Publishers, 1906. "Portrait and autograph of Charles I. "From an engraving after the painting by Sir Anthony Vandyck."

2.1 Picture of Pride's Purge, when General Pride "purged" many members of Parliament from their seats. From *Oliver Cromwell*, by Theodore Roosevelt. New York: Charles Scribner's Sons, 1900. "Pride's Purge."

2.2 Portrait of Edmund Calamy, one of the authors of *Smectymnuus*, as well as a very active member of the

Westminster Assembly and personal friend to Manton. From *The History of the Puritans: Or Protestant Nonconformists from the Reformation in 1517 to the Revolution in 1618*, by Daniel Neal, vol. 2. New York: Harper & Brothers, 1843. "Engraved by Gimber from an Original."

2.3 Picture inside Westminster Hall, where Charles I was tried and sentenced to death. From *Oliver Cromwell*, by Theodore Roosevelt. New York: Charles Scribner's Sons, 1900. "Interior of Westminster Hall."

3.1 Portrait of John Owen, a contemporary of Manton's who was a congregationalist. From *The History of the Puritans: Or Protestant Nonconformists from the Reformation in 1517 to the Revolution in 1618*, by Daniel Neal, vol. 1. New York: Harper & Brothers, 1843. "Engraved by Gimber from an Original Painted in 1656."

3.2 Picture of Charles II, whom Manton (and others) invited to return to become King of England in 1660. From *A History of the American People*, by Woodrow Wilson, vol. 1. New York and London: Harper & Brothers Publishers, 1906. "From a print after the painting by Sir Peter Lely."

3.3 Portrait of William III, who became the King of England with his wife Mary in 1689. From *A History of the American People*, by Woodrow Wilson, vol. 1. New York and London: Harper & Brothers Publishers, 1906. "Portrait and autograph of William III from an old print."

4.1 Portrait of Martin Luther by his friend Lucas Cranach. From *Martin Luther: The Hero of the Reformation 1483–1546*, by Henry Jacobs. New York and London: G. P. Putnam's Sons, 1898. "Luther."

4.2 Portrait of John Calvin, the famous Protestant theologian of Geneva. From *A History of the American People*, by Woodrow Wilson, vol. 1. New York and London: Harper & Brothers Publishers, 1906. Engraved by T. Woolnoth from a painting by Hans Holbein. "John Calvin."

5.1 Title page of Manton's Commentary. From *The Complete Works of Thomas Manton, D.D.*, vol. 4. London: James Nisbet & Co., 1871.

6.1 Map of Virginia in the seventeenth century, where the Teackles lived. From *A History of the American People*, by Woodrow Wilson, vol. 1. New York and London: Harper & Brothers Publishers, 1906. From an original in the New York Public Library engraved by W. Hole. "Captain John Smith's Map of Virginia, 1612."

6.2 Title page for Luther's *The Babylonian Captivity of the Church*, where he attacks the seven sacraments. From *Martin Luther: The Hero of the Reformation 1483–1546*, by Henry Jacobs. New York and London: G. P. Putnam's Sons, 1898. "Luther."

6.3 Title page of the Authorized Version (KJV), which was used by countless theologians like Hammond. From *A History of the American People*, by Woodrow Wilson, vol. 1. New York and London: Harper & Brothers Publishers, 1906. "Title-page of the Royal Version or King James's Bible."

7.1 Portrait of Richard Baxter, a friend and colleague of Manton's. From *The History of the Puritans: Or Protestant Nonconformists from the Reformation in 1517 to the Revolution* *in 1618*, by Daniel Neal, vol. 1. New York: Harper & Brothers, 1843. "Engraved by Gimber from an Original."

8.1 Portrait of Oliver Cromwell, who ruled England during the 1650s. From *Oliver Cromwell*, by Theodore Roosevelt. New York: Charles Scribner's Sons, 1900. "Oliver Cromwell."

9.1 Medal of Ulrich Zwingli, the first Reformer to preach verse-by-verse on Sundays, rather than following the liturgy. From *Martin Luther: The Hero of the Reformation 1483–1546*, by Henry Jacobs. New York and London: G. P. Putnam's Sons, 1898. "Memorial of His Death."

INDEX OF SUBJECTS AND NAMES

Act of Supremacy, 168
Act of Uniformity, 66–67, 69, 210
adversity, 177
affections, 147, 158
ambition, 196
analogy of faith, 103–4, 105–6, 111, 117–20
analogy of Scripture, 106
Anglicanism, resurgence of, 62
Anglo-Catholicism, 25
anointing with oil, 125–30, 138
antilegomena, 90
Apologeticall Declaration, 53
Aristotelianism, 29
Arminians, 25, 26, 140
Augustine, 108–9
auricular confession, 131–33, 137

Barlow, Thomas, 34–35
Bates, William, 15, 59, 66, 70, 72, 74, 76
Baxter, Richard, 11, 16, 40, 60, 63, 64–65, 69, 72, 74, 76, 137–38, 145, 167
Bede, 96
Bedford, James, 70
Belgic Confession, 91, 99
bishops, 125, 136, 138
Bishops' War, 37

Blundell, Peter, 22–23
Bodleian library, 34–35
Bolam, C. G., 65, 68
Book of Common Prayer, 48, 65, 192
Breda, 63–64
Bremer, Francis, 62
Brodrick, George, 30–31
Brooks, Thomas, 192–93
Bull, George, 111
Bullinger, Heinrich, 192
Bunyan, John, 69, 75
Butler, Samuel, 23

Cajetan, Thomas, 83, 86–87, 96–97, 128
Calamy, Edmund, 36, 51, 53, 62, 65
Calvin, John, 55, 58, 83–84, 94, 96, 191, 213
    on anointing, 129
    on auricular confession, 131–32
    on elders, 125
    on extreme unction, 130
    on James, 89–93, 99
Cambridge University, 26
canon, 103
    fluidity of, 90–91, 95, 99–100
    positively and negatively regarded, 92
carnal things, 203

carnal wisdom, 201–2
Cartwright, Thomas, 167
Catholics, 25
Cavalier Parliament, 66, 69
cavaliers, 43
chance, 185
Charles I, 19, 24–25, 37–38, 47, 135, 168, 212
    execution of, 52–53
Charles II, 16, 21, 42–43, 53, 59, 62–65, 69, 71, 73, 141, 168, 169, 212
Chilcott, Robert, 23
Christian life, 92–93, 192
Christian unity, 183–84
church, unity of, 65, 70
church and state, 170
Church of England, 21, 24–25, 35, 48, 57
Church of Scotland, 60
Cicero, 30
civil interests, 202–4
civil magistrate, 170, 189
Clarendon Code, 69
classics, 30
classis movement, 52, 58, 75, 141, 213
Collins, John, 72
Colyton, 46
Commonwealth, 21, 62
comprehension into Church of England, 63, 68, 70–71, 74–76, 137
conformity, 68–69
congregationalists, 24, 47, 60
constitutional monarchy, 43
Conventicle Act, 70
Convention Parliament, 63
Cooper, William, 35
Corporation Act, 69
Costello, William, 29
Council of Trent, 99

Covent Garden, London, 36, 59–64, 67–68, 71–72, 141, 213
covetousness, 196
Cripplegate, 72
Cromwell, Oliver, 16, 21, 49, 53, 59–60, 62, 141, 168–70
Cromwell, Richard, 21, 59, 62, 169
curates, 41

David, 152–53
deacon, 35–36
Declaration of Breda, 63–64
Declaration of Indulgence, 71–72
Directory for Public Worship of God, 48
dissenters, 68–69
divine right of monarchs, 43
dons, 70
ducklings, 71
duty, 163

earthly and heavenly things, 176
Edward VI, King, 23
Edwards, Jonathan, 142, 147
elders, 125, 136, 138, 140
Elizabeth I, 23
English Civil War, 21, 24–25, 42, 46, 49, 56, 62, 170
English Reformation, 168
envy, 196
episcopacy
    corruptions of, 50–51
    reduced, 137
episcopalians, 24, 36
Erasmus, 29, 83, 86–87, 96
established church, 71
Estcot, Daniel, 32
esteem in the world, 202
Estius, Gulielmus, 139–40
eternal death, 174

eternal life, 174
Eusebius, 87, 91, 96–97
Evelyn, John, 61
Exeter College (Oxford), 26
extreme unction, 86, 121,
        123–30, 136, 139–40

faith, 182–83
    exercise of, 178–80
    fruits of, 117
    lively vs. dead, 107–9
    true vs. false, 115
fame, 202
family, 203
Feingold, Mordechai, 28–29, 30
First Conventicle Act, 69
Five Mile Act, 69
Fleetwood, William, 61
flesh, 196
flesh and spirit, 174–75, 187
foolish curiosity, 177
Form of Presbyterial Church
        Government, 48
Fourth Lateran Council, 132
freelance clergymen, 41
friends, 202–3

Gamble, Harry, 91
Gill, John, 142
Glorious Revolution, 74
God
    as chiefest good, 200
    as first cause, 199–200
    as highest lord, 200–201
    justice of, 175–76
    as last end, 201
    sovereignty, 186
    wisdom on, 175–76
godliness, 148
good and evil, 175, 182
Goodwin, Thomas, 60
good works, 107–9

Grand Remonstrance, 42
Great Ejection, 67, 210
Grotius, Hugo, 96, 125, 135

habit of faith, 112
Hagen, Kenneth, 93
Hall, Joseph, 22–23, 36, 51
Hammond, Henry, 123, 133–38,
        141–42
Harris, William, 16, 22, 35–36,
        39, 57, 69, 80
Hart Hall (Oxford), 32–33
healing, 140
heart, and meditation, 165
Heath, William, 49
heaven, 174
hell, 174
Helvetic Confession, 91, 99
Hemmingsen, Niels, 84, 93–95,
        98–99, 130
Henchman, Humphrey, 69
Henry, Matthew, 142
Henry VIII, 168
Hill, Christopher, 19
holy commmonwealth, 170
homologoumena, 90
Horace, 30
Hyde, Edward, 69

idolatry, 194–95, 197–98
Ignatius, 136
independents, 24, 44, 47
instructional meditation, 157
Interregnum, 135, 141
Irish Catholics, 47
Isaac, 148–49, 153–54

James (letter of), 80–82
    as "epistle of straw," 84, 86–90
    Manton's commentary on, 55–57
    reconciliation with Paul,
        114–17, 118–19

James I, 24
James II, 73, 74
Jenkyn, William, 72
Jerome, 87, 89, 91, 96–97
Johnson, Luke Timothy, 17, 87, 121, 145
Jude, Manton's commentary on, 55–57, 80
justification, 101–3
  before God, 112, 114, 116
  before humanity, 112, 114, 116
  by faith, 88, 118, 120
  and works, 87–88, 106

Karlstadt, Andreas von, 89
Knapp, Henry, 105–6, 117–18

language, 30
Latin, 22, 23, 30, 35
Laud, William, 25–26, 30, 47, 60, 170
Leigh, Edward, 104, 109–12, 119, 130
Locke, John, 35, 48
locus method of biblical exegesis, 106
logic, 29
Lombard, Peter, 128
London, 48–49
Long Parliament, 38, 42–44, 46–48, 50, 170
Lotz, David, 88
Louis XIV, 71
love, 161–62
Love, Christopher, 53–54, 170
lust, 196–97
Luther, Martin, 148, 168
  on canon, 92
  on extreme unction, 126–27
  on James, 83–89, 96–100, 103, 120
  on justification by faith, 101, 118

magisterial reformers, 168
Maller, Charles, 30
Manton, Thomas
  on auricular confession, 131–33
  as chaplain, 169–70
  death of, 74–77
  on extreme unction, 123–30
  imprisonment of, 70
  on James, 55–57, 80–82, 84–85, 95–100, 123
  on Jude, 80
  on justification, 112–17
  lecturer at Sowton, 41
  on meditating, 147–65
  as moderate and cooperative, 60
  as nonconformist, 68–74
  as pastor, 212–13
  as peacekeeper, 74–77
  as preacher, 42, 75, 143–44, 212–13
  preaching before Parliament, 50–51, 58, 170, 213
  as presbyterian, 75, 137
  as public theologian, 214–16
  as Puritan, 12, 210–12
  reception in America, 122–23, 142
  at Westminster Assembly, 49, 75
  works of, 217–21
Manton, Thomas (father), 22
Marshall, Stephen, 51
Mary I, Queen, 23
Mary, Queen of Scots, 24
material possessions, 202
Mather, Cotton and Increase, 122, 142
Mayer, John, 104–9, 119, 130
meditation, 145–47
  and the heart, 165
  as a middle duty, 163–65
  vs. study, 147
Melanchthon, Philip, 95

mercies, 186
mixed providences, 172–85
modified episcopalianism, 64–65
monarchy, 43,
    reestablishment of, 53, 63
Monck, George, 62–63
Morgan, Mary (wife), 41
mortification, 197
Moses, 150–51
Muller, Richard, 83, 90, 135,
    139

Newcomen, Matthew, 51
New Model Army, 44
Nisbet, James, 209
nonconformists, 142

occasional meditation, 156, 165
O'Day, Rosemary, 27, 35
Oecumenius, 107–9
Old, Hughes Oliphant, 17, 81
ordination, of Thomas Manton,
    36
Ovid, 30
Owen, John, 11, 16, 22, 32,
    34–35, 40, 48–49, 60, 70,
    72, 75, 212
Oxford Oath, 70
Oxford University, 25–35

Packer, J. I., 145
Paraeus, David, 107–8
parish, 40
Parliament, 38
parliamentarians, 43
patience, 184
Patrick, Simon, 68–69
Pemble, William, 108, 110
Perkins, William, 58, 67, 101,
    106, 192, 213
Petrarch, 30
Pinners' Hall, 71

Polycarp, 136
Poole, Matthew, 74, 141–42
Popham, Alexander, 48–49
Porter, Stanley, 39–40
Porter, Stephen, 26–27
practical biblical exposition, 17
practical meditation, 157–58
praise, 205–6
prayer, 129, 205–6
    and meditation, 163–65
preaching
    continuously through
        Scripture, 55–56
    in Reformed tradition, 191–92
presbyterianism, 49, 50–52, 58,
    137, 213
    defeat of, 65, 67–68
presbyterians, 24, 44, 47, 62, 70
present life, 174
Pride's Purge, 44, 52, 62
prophecy, preaching as, 192
prosperity, 177
Protectorate, 21, 141
proto-Anglicans, 24
providence, 172–85, 200–201
Puritans, 11, 16–17, 24, 44, 47,
    103, 121
    on analogy of faith, 105, 117–20
    as anti-Laud, 25
    loss of public voice, 142
    marginalization of, 210–12, 216
    as Reformed Catholic, 212
    use of Manton, 122–23

Quakers, 68
Queen's College (Oxford), 32,
    35
quidrivium, 30

Ramism, 29
reason, and analogy of faith, 111
rectors, 41

religious toleration, 60
Renaissance, 29–30
Restoration, 47, 56, 62, 137–38,
    168, 210
revenge, 184
Reynolds, Edward, 66
rhetoric, 29
Richardson, Caroline, 74
righteousness, 201
Roman Catholics, 71, 72–74
    on Eucharist, 191–92
"roundheads," 43
royalists, 43, 63
Royal Society, 61
Rump Parliament, 52
Russell, William, 60
Ryle, J. C., 15, 34, 167, 209–12,
    214–15, 217

Savoy Conference, 66
scope, 113, 119–20
Scotland, 37–38, 43
Scottish Covenanters, 47–48
Scripture, meditation on,
    145–47
Scudamore, Ruth, 110
Second Helvetic Confession, 192
Sedgwick, Obadiah, 60
self-denial, 193–207
self-love, 198–99
self-will, 200
Seneca, 30, 148
Sheldon, Gilbert, 66
Short Parliament, 38, 42
sin, and sickness, 130–31,
    135–36
Skarsten, Tyrgve, 94
Smectymnuus Redivivus, 51
social issues, Manton on, 58, 213
sola scriptura, 124
Solemn League and Covenant,
    48, 67

solemn meditation, 156–57, 165
Somerset, 22, 26
Sowton, 41
spiritual gifts, cessation of,
    129–30
Spurgeon, C. H., 15, 19
Spurr, John, 65–66, 68–69, 71, 74
Spurstowe, William, 51
standing ordinance, 126–30
St. John, Oliver, 61
St. Mary's church (Stoke
    Newington), 49
Stoke Newington, 48–49, 55–58,
    61, 96, 213
Stone, Lawrence, 27
St. Paul's (Covent Garden),
    60–64, 141, 211
study, 147, 158

Teackle, Thomas, 122, 142
Tertullian, 130
thankfulness, 186
Thiemann, Ron, 214
Thirty-Nine Articles of Religion,
    47–48, 67
Thoresby, Ralph, 42, 59, 75–76
Tiverton, 22–23
Toon, Peter, 63, 71, 76
trivium, 30
Trueman, Carl, 24n2, 121, 123,
    210, 212
tutors, at Oxford, 31–32
Tyacke, Nicholas, 28

undergraduate curriculum,
    28–31
university education, 27
unwritten traditions, 124
Usher, James, 61, 65, 74, 137

vicars, 41
Virgil, 30

Wadham College (Oxford), 26–28, 31–32, 34
Wadham, Nicholas, 26
Watson, Thomas, 11
Watts, Michael, 63, 72
Westminster Abbey, 60
Westminster Assembly, 21, 46–49, 75
Westminster Confession of Faith, 16, 39, 48, 98–100, 141
Westminster Larger Catechism, 48

Westminster Shorter Catechism, 48
Whitby, Daniel, 123, 137–42
Whiting, Charles, 67
William and Mary, 74
will of God, 200
Wood, Anthony, 23, 32–33
Wood, Harold, 74
Word, and meditation, 163–64

Young, Thomas, 51

Zwingli, Ulrich, 55, 168, 191

INDEX OF SCRIPTURE

Genesis
24:63—148

Psalms
119—79

Isaiah
53—56, 79, 193

Zechariah
14:6–7—170–71
14:9—50

Matthew
7:1—41
16:24—193
25—79

John
17—79

Romans
6—79
8—79

1 Corinthians
3:10–15—88

2 Corinthians
5—80

Philippians
2:27—139

2 Thessalonians
2—79

Hebrews
11—80
12:1—67

James
1—82
1:1—96
2:14–26—82, 98
2:15–26—103–20, 124
2:24—101
5:14–16—82, 121–42

1 Peter
4:10–11—140

Revelation
3:20—50
3:28—101, 107